A practical guide for parents, carers and grandparents
to identify and nurture children's gifts and talents

Find and Nurture Your Child's Gifts

Boost your Child's Learning Potential and Wellbeing (4 to 11 years)

by

Professor Valsa Koshy
and
Dr Elizabeth Koshy

A professor of education and a medical doctor answer the questions:
How do we find our children's gifts?
How do we nurture our children's gifts to realise their full potential?

First published in the United Kingdom in 2017 by enrichchildrenslives.

Copyright © 2017 Valsa Koshy and Elizabeth Koshy.

The information contained in this book is based on many years of experience of working in education and medicine and is only intended for the reader. We use published evidence and policy documents to illustrate the ideas and guidance we have included. We would like to highlight that no single book can provide all that parents, carers and grandparents need to know. The reader may need to seek further professional guidance for a specific issue, if required.

ISBN 978-1900905-15-2

Cover design by Andrew Hill

Typeset by Natalie White

Printed and bound by Victoire Press Limited

Testimonials

This book presents a powerful and unique perspective on how to maximise children's talents, regardless of their economic or social background. The emphasis is on spotting and developing children's early interests and passions, and on using them as strong motivators for happiness and success. The authors emphasise that all children can thrive, given the right opportunities and encouragement. Following the simple guidance in this book, parents, grandparents and carers, can make a difference to their lives.

As someone who came through childhood trauma and the care system but who found early inspiration and confidence from playing chess, I myself recognise the benefits of the authors' approach. And for me, it only took one or two adults who cared and noticed, to make a big difference, so I know it can work.

Richard Farleigh
A highly successful businessman and investor,
Ambassador for Action for Children, Chancellor at London South Bank University and
former investor on the Dragons' Den BBC2 TV programme

This book is an excellent guide for parents of young children. Parents will find the chapters on promoting mental health in children, and dealing with problems in areas such as sleep and diet, particularly useful. Being a parent in the modern world is stressful. Families are now more dispersed and the support and advice that parents may have received from their relatives in the era when family members lived close together is now long over for many people. Parents do though still need clear, authoritative, evidence-based and readable guidance on parenting. This book provides that and will be a very valuable addition to every household with young children.

Professor Azeem Majeed
GP and Head of the Department of Primary Care and Public Health at Imperial College London

I have known Professor Koshy for over 14 years, firstly as a mentor for teaching gifted and talented mathematicians, before becoming my supervisor for my Master's, then doctorate degree. She has inspired me to further my education, as well as developing my passion for ensuring the most able pupils I am responsible for are properly educated.

Professor Koshy's books are always equally inspirational to teachers. She has the knack of demystifying complex concepts and making difficult pedagogy appear really quite simple. In her research work, she has often included the views of parents, and from my own research I have learnt that parents provide a different and very important perspective on their child's abilities.

It seems a perfectly logical next step for Professor Koshy to write a book for parents about nurturing their child's gifts. This book makes me realise what a gap in the market there has been for this resource for parents, because nobody cares more about nurturing a child's gifts than his or her own parents. Furthermore, this is a book for all parents, because, as Professor Koshy explains in the book, intelligence is not fixed, and all children can achieve given the right opportunities and motivation. Reading this book, parents will learn something of the academic background about how to provide optimally for children to develop their abilities. Then Professor Koshy provides practical ideas about ways to inspire children to challenge themselves.

A unique feature of this book is the collaboration with Dr Elizabeth Koshy, and the importance of physical and mental wellbeing as a prerequisite for good learning. As a headteacher of an inner-city primary school, I know only too well how difficult it is for children to focus on learning when there are far more basic needs to be met. The sections on both mental and physical health reflect the current challenges that both the education and health sectors are struggling with daily. Connecting the two issues in the manner here underscores the importance of looking at the whole child.

I know I shall be recommending this book to the parents at my school – involving parents in their children's education is known to be a great way to accelerate children's outcomes. I know that parents will be thoroughly reassured and inspired when they read this book.

Dr Margaret Brady
Headteacher, St Paul's Primary School, Walworth

Parenting is tough. And most of us have no training except our own experience of our parents! Great if they did a good job, but tough if they, like most of us, got it wrong to a lesser or greater degree.

There is great advice here on developing our kids' ability. Perhaps even more important is the guidance to help us grow happiness, security and resilience in our children – something we would all give anything to achieve. The good news is it's not expensive to accomplish and is something we can all afford! Sensible, clear, attainable ideas are here to assist us. Even better they are based on good evidence in an era where so much information is pure opinion or prejudice. Happily, the evidence does not get in the way of reading the book easily and is there for us to look into further if that's our bent. Well worth reading or dipping into to encourage us in the most rewarding and most challenging task we can possibly face – being a great mum or dad.

Dr Phil Moore
GP, Clinical Co-Director for Mental Health NHS England (London), Chair Mental Health Commissioners Network of NHS Clinical Commissioners

There are additional testimonials at the back of the book.

Dedications

Valsa: I dedicate this book to my husband.

Elizabeth: I dedicate this book to my parents and my own family.

Contents

About the Authors

The co-authors of this book are mother and daughter.

Professor Valsa Koshy BSc, MA, MPhil, PhD

Valsa Koshy founded the first university-based Centre for Talent Development at Brunel University, in 1996, to support teachers, educationists and parents to identify and nurture children's potential.

The unique feature of her work has been celebrating both academic excellence in children and at the same time recognising multiple gifts and talents with the ultimate aim of helping children to reach their full potential irrespective of their background. She encourages us to ask, 'What are my child's gifts and talents?' rather than, 'Is my child gifted?' She has written 18 books on talent development and mathematics education. She has also published widely in international academic journals and has made over 30 conference presentations, including at the American Education Research Association (AERA) conference and at the British Educational Research Association (BERA) conferences. In her academic career she has taught trainee teachers, led extensive professional development courses and was responsible for a Masters degree in Gifted Education. She has also supervised several national and international PhD doctoral students, many of whom researched areas related to gifted education.

Prior to embarking on an academic career, she was a teacher and a member of the advisory team for the Inner London Education Authority (ILEA) for mathematics.

The work Valsa is most proud of is founding the Urban Scholars Programme, aimed at raising the aspirations and achievement of teenagers who live in challenging circumstances and following up their subsequent journeys towards happy and successful lives. She has directed a significant number of research and development projects for the UK government and several charities.

Valsa feels fortunate to be a professor. However, for any readers who may think hers was an easy journey from the beginning, it was not. She was a 'disaster' as a child and, to her parents' dismay and horror, she was temporarily suspended from school when she was 13 years old, for not conforming to structured school tasks and for following creative and alternative interpretations to tasks within the school. That gives hope for all children and parents!

Dr Elizabeth Koshy BSc, MBBS, DRCOG, MRCGP (Distinction), MSc, PhD

Elizabeth has worked as a general practitioner (GP), a course lead responsible for the delivery of a general practice course to medical undergraduate students, a postgraduate tutor and a medical researcher at Imperial College London. She also obtained her PhD in Medicine from Imperial College London. She is a mother, which, she views, is the most challenging, but rewarding, role she has ever undertaken! In this book, she follows one of her great passions of helping parents to create the right foundations to boost children's wellbeing and learning potential, to help towards achieving almost every parent's and grandparent's dream for their children and grandchildren, to lead happy, healthy and successful lives.

Her passion for helping children was ignited at medical school, when she won prizes relating to paediatrics and child health. For instance, she was one of only two medical students, in her cohort year, to obtain a Royal College of Paediatrics and Child Health prize during her final year at medical school. Elizabeth worked as a junior doctor in hospitals and then in general practice. She obtained a distinction from the Royal College of General Practitioners for her 'Membership of the Royal College of General Practitioners' (MRCGP) examinations. She completed an MSc in Epidemiology and then obtained a PhD degree in Medicine from Imperial College London. She has been awarded national prizes and competitive national research fellowships.

Being a mother, doctor, undergraduate and postgraduate tutor and medical researcher, have all contributed to her being able to provide an overview and varied perspective on children's wellbeing and external factors which influence whether children realise their potential. She also fully appreciates that theory is never easy to put into practice!

Elizabeth worked as a GP in affluent and also very deprived areas, and has seen a range of physical and psychosocial problems among children from different socio-economic backgrounds. She has seen countless children who were stressed and anxious, frequently because of fear of failure in tests and social problems. This has made her passionate about raising awareness about anxiety and stress among children and offering help and guidance.

Elizabeth was still at school herself when her parents first became involved in the area of gifted education and she was exposed to their developing ideas. She became fascinated by their conversations and discussions and became increasingly interested in the field and concepts of giftedness herself. Many conversations in the sitting room turned into topics relating to IQ and specific talents of famous people and generated much discussion!

Acknowledgements

Valsa Koshy

I am indebted to many people who have supported me on my journey to this point, to have the confidence to write a book for parents. They have facilitated my learning and research about the different aspects of ability and how to spot and develop children's special abilities and talents, which is at the heart of all my work. It is impossible for me to list all the people who have influenced me and supported me over the years and I would like to express my gratitude to all of them. Especially, I would like to thank: Professor Linda Thomas and Professor Steve Hodkinson, who helped to launch both the Research and Development Centre, studying aspects of high ability, in 1996 and the Urban Scholars Programme for tackling disadvantage of teenagers, at Brunel University. I thank Professor Mansoor Sarhadi, the former Vice Principal for helping me to make my mission to make a difference to children's lives a reality.

I am extremely grateful to Professor Julia Buckingham, the Vice Chancellor, Professor William Leahy and Professor Andrew George, Deputy Vice Chancellors at Brunel University, and the senior management team at Brunel University for providing a fertile ground to nurture and grow my ideas. My sincere gratitude to Professor Thomas Betteridge for his support. I especially value his appreciation of the role of the human dimension and compassion within Education. The support from Professor Susan Capel, my former Head of School, Jac Aldous and Genevieve Dewez has been invaluable in fulfilling my desire to make a difference to the practical aspects of supporting children who live in challenging circumstances. Professor Charles Desforges of Exeter University, who has been my mentor and supporter for many years. His reassurance that I was doing something with significant benefit has always meant a great deal to me. He taught me how to carry out research that enhances the quality of children's lives. Andrea Masters, personal Assistant to the Vice Principal at Brunel University, for her continued support for my work and for constantly reminding me that what I was doing was worthwhile. I owe her considerable gratitude. Gary Dear, our finance officer, who made sure that my projects ran smoothly by going that extra mile to offer his support. I am grateful to Professor Viv Ellis and Dr Cathy Gower, as well as to past and present colleagues in the Education Department. I am also indebted to the Urban Scholars Programme team – Carole Portman Smith, Catherina Emery and Linda McPhee for their continued support and encouragement. Much gratitude also goes to Jane Alexander, our Departmental Administrator, for sharing my passion for fairness and social justice. Eileen Runkel, who has worked with me for many years and has read the manuscript of this book and offered practical and constructive advice. I am extremely grateful to Dr Yvonne Perret for the encouragement and support she has given me over many years. I have really appreciated David Ward's help – particularly his reliability and attention to detail. We are very grateful to Jennifer Clark and Natalie White for their help to prepare the manuscript. Most importantly, all the teachers and parents I have met and worked with. I have seen, first-hand, their level of enthusiasm, excitement and commitment to do the best for their children. Also, the many children I have worked with over 20 years – both at Brunel University and in schools – in my efforts to support them in nurturing their special gifts and talents. Those were magical moments.

Elizabeth Koshy

I would like to express my gratitude for the support that the following people have given me. My family. My parents for always encouraging, but never pushing me and my whole family for their understanding and support. Colleagues and friends in my different roles in hospitals, general practice (particularly at my wonderful training practices) and academia. I have learnt a great deal about people and life during the journey. It was during this time of meeting hundreds of people – countless patients, as well as my peers, seniors and juniors – that truly helped me to develop my emotional intelligence skills and the ability to see beyond the surface and really *suss* people out! This has been the most valuable lesson I have learnt in my life. The children and parents I saw in my role as a medical doctor, and in meetings alongside Valsa, had a particular impact on me and my thinking. I am grateful to numerous people at Imperial College London and too many for me to mention everyone, but I am particularly indebted to Professor Azeem Majeed, for his immense knowledge and wisdom, tremendous support and encouragement during my different teaching and research roles over a 10-year period. I am extremely grateful to Dr Phil Moore, whose knowledge, integrity and compassion really inspired me. I am immensely appreciative of my wonderful friends and particularly my closest ones – Jules, Jojo and Hannah – for genuine, unconditional friendship and tremendous loyalty over many years. They always enhance my wellbeing! I am also extremely grateful to the following people who have been there for me when I needed them professionally or personally: Frances, Jo, Norma, Gerald, Peter, Kate, George, Neal, Jean, Natasha, Simon, Charlotte, Al, Claire, Lucy, Muriel, Ann, Amanda, Steve, Ginny, Derek, Diane, Eric, Sonia, Alex, Mike, Farzan, Javier, Jenna, Christine, Fiona, Eszter, Ela, Pirkko, Kit, Lizzie, Norma, Barbara, Doli, Alex, Josip, Lizzie, Alon, Caroline, Margot, Justin, Rosie, Khatim, Mel, Louise, Amanda, Anne and Natalie. Many apologies to anyone

I have inadvertently omitted. Finally, I am eternally grateful to the National Institute for Health Research for funding two research fellowships.

A string of challenging events during my life, in childhood and then in adulthood, as well as meeting certain, key people over time, have spurred me to re-evaluate life and people. This has led me to follow a personal and passionate pathway to understand and improve the wellbeing of children – to help children and their carers strive towards happier lives. Becoming a mother has taught me that wellbeing is the foundation for almost everything a child does. I have witnessed, at first-hand, that positive wellbeing is a prerequisite for learning, while negative or poor wellbeing can have the converse effect.

Foreword

Until recently, very little was known in an objective sense about children, childhood, child rearing or parenting. Plenty of people had very strong views on all these matters but for most folk, child rearing was a matter of custom and practice – a set of taken for granted cultural habits. In contrast, a modern parent is faced with a vast and ever increasing amount of scientific research on all aspects of education and childrearing including diet, sleep, wellbeing and health. In this book, the authors discuss relevant and useful information from the mine of literature available and make it accessible and practical for the reader.

Again, until recently, a child's birth was its destiny. Farmers' children would labour in fields and fisher-folk children would go to sea. In contrast, over recent decades, vast opportunities have opened up for most children in the developed world. Two hundred years ago, a central question in a parent's mind would have been, 'How soon can I put this child to gainful employment?' Nowadays a more common question is, 'How can I help my child to make the most of their potential?' These positions are gross generalisations of course. There are many parents who do not think ahead for themselves or their children but it is safe to assume that since you have read thus far you are not such a parent. You are already considering how to help your child make the best of themselves.

You will not be short of advice. There are zealots (e.g. 'Tiger Moms' who are very proud of their parenting and who urge you to follow their scripts). There are ideologues who have strong philosophical or religious or political views on how children should be raised to develop into a pre-ordained specification of ideal adulthood. Here in your hand you have a different approach – a source of information relevant to parenting gathered by Valsa and Elizabeth Koshy and based on the best available scientific studies of childhood and child development. They cover a range of matters including education, learning, thinking, diet, physical and mental health. The authors use their studies to address key parenting questions as these arise in a modern setting. How do I build my child's intellectual strengths to enhance their learning and creativity? How do I help my child to be physically and mentally strong? How much sleep does my child need? What is a good diet and how do I get my child to eat such?

The authors are scientists and so are well able to explain the relevant research. They are also mothers and a grandparent. They know how difficult the 'real world' can be and so the science is presented with wisdom and humility. In addition, they take a 'whole child' approach. Your child is not an eater, a sleeper, a learner and so on. Your child is a person. Your child is not a blank sheet of paper on which you can write your script. Your child has their own nature with which you have to learn to interact.

I am reminded here of my own childhood. My elder sister taught me to read, write and to do basic arithmetic before I went to school. I never looked back. My sister completely failed to teach my younger brother anything because, as she put it, 'he would not sit still long enough'. We boys had very different natures. I was an anxious introvert. He was a cheerful extravert. Whilst we inhabited the same material environment our experience of it was completely different. To him, a bicycle was a golden opportunity to go places. To me a bike was an existential threat. I travelled further (and safer) in a book. Everyone treated my brother with great bonhomie. Everyone treated me with the scepticism with which I treated them. Nature reacts with nurture in two-way interaction. My brother and I both became successful in our chosen work because everyone helped us make the best of who we already were.

Good parents recognise the individuality of children. Parenting is a performing art. It can be well informed or ignorant and clumsy. Valsa and Elizabeth Koshy offer you, in this book, the best possible information base on which to play your role.

Professor Charles Desforges, OBE

Author of The Impact of Parental Involvement, Parental Support and Family Education on Pupil Achievement and Adjustment: A Literature Review. Research carried out for the UK Department of Education and Skills, 2003.
Former Director of the Teaching and Learning Research Programme of the Economic and Social Research Council (ESRC)
Former Deputy Vice Chancellor and Director of the School of Education, University of Exeter

Preface

A Family Affair – Join Us in Our Journey of Exploration and Our Learning Along the 'Gifted and Talented' Highway

Valsa Koshy

Many teachers and parents ask me how I became interested in this area and about our family's *journey*. If you are interested in hearing this too, please read on. However, if you would like to skip this, I will not be at all offended, and please go straight to the next section, 'Terminology and Purpose of this Book'.

How it all Started

It was 1987. I was invited to lead a workshop at an Inner London Education Authority (ILEA) conference on gifted children. I did not consider myself an expert and was nervous, but I prepared well for the event and was encouraged by the interest and feedback from the delegates that I had delivered a 'very good session'. I decided that giftedness in children was an area of study worth spending time on and delving into, on a much deeper level. The publicity that followed this 'first of its kind' conference organised by the then largest education authority raised quite a lot of attention from schools, journalists and voluntary organisations.

Gradually, I realised that highly able children, or whatever terms we use to describe them – gifted, bright, very able, or talented – deserved to be supported to fulfil their potential. This realisation led me to accept an invitation to run a Saturday programme for young, gifted children, provided by an organisation for gifted children. The level of interest in the whole topic was high and this helped to provide us with an opportunity to actually work with children (5–11 years) who were selected to attend the classes. Some children and parents travelled up to 60 miles to attend the classes and my whole family became involved in supporting the children. We offered children a range of activities – including mathematics, creative writing, personal research topics and quizzes. The level of enthusiasm from both the children and the parents was so remarkable that we found the whole experience very enjoyable and rewarding. One of the features that interested us during this time was that all the children were IQ tested and obtained a high enough score to qualify to attend the classes. All the children who attended the classes were who teachers would describe as 'bright'. However, their interests and aptitudes were different. This intrigued me and raised some questions in my mind:

What defines a gifted child?

Is only someone with a high IQ gifted?

Are there common attributes that make gifted children different?

More Questions than Answers

As word circulated around local schools about what I was doing, I received phone calls from parents of primary school children asking if I could help them. Spurred on by Elizabeth, my daughter and co-author of this book, who had by now become very interested in the whole concept of giftedness and selection of children, we agreed to meet families and give practical advice using my experience as a teacher, a member of the ILEA advisory team and, by then, a university lecturer, teaching undergraduates and supporting practising teachers.

Meeting Maria and Jason

We met Jason, who was 7-years old, and his mother, Maria. Maria explained to us that she had noticed some of Jason's behaviours, which led her to believe that her son was gifted. She described these *behaviours* as taking an interest in weather forecasting from 4-years old and comparing it at the end of the day to see how accurate it was, an exceptional memory which helped him to win board games and so on. Maria, with our support and encouragement, approached her son's teacher to share her experiences, which the teacher received very positively. During our conversations, we also discovered that Jason's father was in prison for arson and neither parent had completed secondary education. This raised another question for us:

Is aptitude or giftedness dependent on one's background and education?

Working with Ahmed for a BBC Programme

In 1994, an unexpected invitation came from BBC Television asking if I would like to work with them on producing a documentary with the title *Too Clever By Half*. Initially, the intention was that I would talk to Colette Hiller, BBC's consultant to the programme and a very talented journalist. Nervously, in February 1994, I took part in the BBC2 programme *Too Clever By Half*, which featured 6-year-old Ahmed. The BBC programme introduced Ahmed as exceptionally gifted. He lived in a council estate and was, at the time, being educated at home, mainly by his mother. Ahmed's mother felt he was bored at school, as he said that he was 'not learning anything'. Ahmed's IQ was tested by a psychologist and part of the assessment was shown on television. The test showed Ahmed to be exceptionally bright, with a high IQ and very capable in several dimensions. Ahmed's delightful personality and his mother's modesty made them very popular with the tutors at the weekend workshops and the BBC team. From Ahmed's father's wages as a road sweeper, the family paid for one hour's tuition for Ahmed. He was not allowed to play outside on the council estate and his mother taught him mathematics, discussed ideas with him and developed his social skills at home.

Participating in the BBC programme made me determined to dedicate my efforts to studying aspects of educating very bright or high potential children. I found out what schools were doing and started to design practical programmes for teachers. I also explored how parents can support their children to fulfil their potential.

Two questions that regularly arose were:

What can parents do to spot their children's abilities and talents?

How can parents help children to develop these abilities and talents?

These two questions applied to both affluent and well-educated parents whose children were attending high-achieving schools, as well as those whose children attended schools where low achievement and social problems dominated.

A Thought-Provoking Interview with Barry Hugill, *The Observer*

A flurry of media coverage followed the BBC programme and I (still publicity-shy) was interviewed by several newspapers. This interest strengthened my resolve to find out more about giftedness, and how it can be identified and nurtured. Barry Hugill, then education correspondent at *The Observer* newspaper, quizzed me on several issues about the topic of gifted children. In his article, he described my views as 'pragmatic' and told me that my thoughts seemed 'different, deeper and more pragmatic'. When I asked him to explain what he meant, he told me – not only had I admitted how difficult the whole subject was, I also showed that I had a social conscience about it all – a drive for fairness, equality and social justice. Barry Hugill made me reflect deeply and we were touched, as a family, and motivated by his comments.

Founding the First University-based Research Centre for Educating Children with High Ability

Following the BBC programme, countless requests came from schools and parents for help. As a result, in 1996, Ron Casey and I set up the first university-based research and development unit in the UK at Brunel University. Government funding, research and conference income have helped towards researching aspects of higher ability for 20 years and providing practical support to teachers and parents.

In 2000, Ron Casey and I launched a flagship Urban Scholars Programme (USP), which was designed to support bright or high potential children from urban schools, many of whom were from poorer families. It was designed to support teenagers from inner-city schools to raise their achievement and aspirations by inviting the children to attend the university once a month on Saturdays for three or four years. This programme has been highly successful, as assessed by external evaluators, and has been running now for 16 years. Much of my learning about how parents can take an active part in both talent spotting and developing their children's talents came from the parents, with whom I have worked on this programme.

Questions, Questions and More Questions

I was asked to participate in a parents' workshop regarding how parents can help their children in both spotting and developing their children's gifts and talents. I discussed the common questions parents usually ask me. Some of these questions will be shared, later in the section, 'Parent Conversations'.

Terminology and Purpose of this Book

Valsa Koshy and Elizabeth Koshy

The Terms We Use in this Book

There are many definitions and interpretations of the words *giftedness* and *talent*. A range of other words, including bright, sharp, top-flight, genius, brilliant, intelligent, advanced for one's age, precocious and clever are also used to describe children and adults who display special aptitudes or abilities. The *Oxford Dictionary* definition of *gifted* is a person having exceptional talent or natural ability.

There is, in fact, no universally accepted definition of being gifted. In this book, we use the terms *gifted, talented* and *highly able* interchangeably. **The description of a *gifted* person that we adopt for this book is a person who displays or shows potential special abilities or aptitudes in any area(s).** We believe that these special abilities need to be nurtured and can be developed if we create the right conditions for their detection and growth.

Our Readers

We have written this book for parents, carers and grandparents. Rather than use the three words each time, we use the term *parents* to refer to all three groups. We also use the words child and children interchangeably within the book.

The Experts and Research

We have included many references to experts in the field of *gifted* education and *talent* development. The research they have done and our own research, together with what we have learnt from our many years of experience are also referred to. If you wish to find out more about the various experts and their contributions, please have a look at the References section at the end of the book. You may also put their names in an internet search engine and find out more about their fascinating work. We hope you enjoy reading our book and remember:

Ask: *What is my child's gift?* instead of asking, *Is my child gifted?*

Parent Conversations

Valsa Koshy and Elizabeth Koshy

Recently, we invited a group of parents to explore their ideas about how to boost their children's learning potential. The parents asked some very interesting questions and conversations took place, all very relevant to the book you are about to read. Typically, the parents were interested to find out more about giftedness among children.

The parents ranged from quite affluent ones to lower income families. Their children were not present during our conversations. Some of the parents were very articulate and confident; others were quite diffident and seemed a little intimidated when they arrived. The discussion started with some parents sharing their viewpoints, indicating the essence of their perceptions of the topic of giftedness in children. We have presented some of their comments here.

- 'I looked up the dictionary. It gives the meaning for giftedness as having exceptional talent or ability. Do children have this at birth or can we develop this?'

- 'Knowing your child has a gift is like knowing where there is a gold-mine. That does not make the gold valuable or make you rich. What is needed are the skills required to bring the gold to the surface and make it into a variety of impressive products.' (This metaphor amused many of the parents.) Other metaphors emerged later.

- 'I read somewhere that some people think certain ethnic groups have inferior intelligence. That's not true, because in my boy's class a boy from an ethnic minority always gets the top marks.'

- 'What irritates me most is when schools have a gifted and talented group of children. What is the difference between the two words and why combine them?'

- 'My 8-year-old daughter is very bright and shows gifts in some areas. But she is often called "stupid" by other children. She is dyslexic and I have heard that children with problems such as a learning difficulty, sight, hearing or other physical problems can be teased or bullied.'

- 'I think this is all because some parents want their child to be part of a mental aristocracy, an upper-class of intelligence. They want their children to be superior to others, like those rich people who own estates and mansions.'

- 'I think it all comes down to having a great memory – that is what giftedness is all about.'

- 'Most gifts need to be unwrapped so they can be enjoyed. Giftedness in children also needs to be unwrapped to be revealed to know what is within and what the features are.'

- 'I have two boys. One is in the gifted and talented group in the school: he works hard and is self-motivated and the other one loves socialising and organising things. I wonder what their life courses will be in terms of success.'

- 'You read about all these youngsters taking exams early and winning competitions. After a few years, you don't hear about what they have actually achieved.'

In addition to the issues raised by the parents' comments above, we have been asked a variety of questions over the years. Take a look at some of these questions below and pause for a few moments and think about how you would answer them. As you read the book you will discover many of the answers. We have also given answers in the final chapter. Don't cheat!

- *Q1:* I am not all that familiar with terms like giftedness, talented, very able and so on. If I don't know these, how can I tell if my child is gifted?

- *Q2:* My friend's child came home with a letter from school saying she is gifted. My son scores much higher marks than this child in mathematics and yet I didn't get a letter.

- *Q3:* My daughter is very disruptive in class, but we find her extremely bright and she responds to challenges at home. What is wrong?

- *Q4:* Our 6-year-old boy is at least four years ahead of the others in his class in mathematics. Why can't the school move him to a class of older children?

- *Q5:* I am often told I must praise my child whenever I can. Recently, I read somewhere that it is not good to just praise children and that I should challenge them.

- *Q6:* My son is gifted. He is a loner and is very unhappy. He tells me he has no friends. What should I do?

- *Q7:* I keep hearing about helping children to think. How do you do that? Isn't that what the school is supposed to do?

- *Q8:* We are a poor family. Neither my husband nor I had a proper education. We left school before we were 16. Are there things we can do to help our daughter, so we can make sure she has better opportunities?

- *Q9:* You often see gifted children being arrogant and looking down on their teachers and peers. Does this always happen?

- *Q10:* Are there any checklists I can use that I can tick to help me decide if my child is gifted?

- *Q11:* Is it good or bad for children to be labelled gifted?

- *Q12:* Does a child have to be gifted in all subjects to be considered a 'gifted child'?

Introduction

Valsa Koshy and Elizabeth Koshy

Why this Book?

Every child has talents. Sometimes they are obvious, sometimes more hidden. Finding and nurturing these talents help your child develop motivation, will-power, self-belief, determination and persistence – often far beyond his or her initial area of interest. If you follow the guidance set out in this book, your child is likely to be more self-confident, happier and accomplished.

We are mother and daughter and this book is based on many years of research and work with parents, teachers and children. We present findings from a number of research studies. However, we also present anecdotal evidence and common sense advice, based on our and others' experiences, because we appreciate that research cannot be directly applied to every aspect of children's lives and because children are not robots!

Who is this Book For?

This book is written for parents (which, as defined earlier, refers to parents, grandparents and carers). All parents want the best for their children, but doing the *best* for children requires understanding, consideration and some effort to steer them in the right direction. Throughout the book, we provide you with ideas and action points on how to achieve this, based on our experience and research. Alongside the ideas, we have included many examples of how parents can nurture and develop their children's various gifts and talents, interests and strengths.

> Many parents switch off when they hear the words gifted and talented because they immediately think of the top 1 in 100 children and cannot imagine that their child might be one of them. However, *every child possesses abilities and our mission is to uncover and nurture them.*

In the next section, we will discuss a possible definition of *giftedness* and you will see that it does not just apply to an *elite* group of children but to every child – including yours! What we invite you to do is not difficult. We give you a set of principles and activities, such as *doing things together, talking together, developing thinking and working together with your child's school*.

Remember:

> ⭐ Your child is unique and every individual child has a strength or interest, and some have many. Both spotting and developing these unique strengths and interests are in your hands. Your child has potential and this potential can be enhanced and turned into higher performance.

Giftedness and Your Child

The words *giftedness* and *talent* are interpreted differently within different social and cultural groups. They may also be interpreted differently by different teachers.

As discussed in the section 'Terminology and Purpose of this Book' earlier, we use a range of words interchangeably. **Our definition for what many call *giftedness* encompasses potential and a capacity to learn.** Children may exhibit their *high ability* in some area earlier or later. Some children with *high ability* may not show any high performance because of external factors, such as social or emotional problems, a learning difficulty, physical disabilities or other special educational needs, or as a result of difficult family circumstances.

Many children have the potential for higher performance and achievement, whether it be academic ability or special aptitudes in other areas, given the right support and encouragement. Undoubtedly, there is a spectrum of ability, with what is frequently described as 'genius' and 'exceptional' at the top end of the spectrum. However, with help and support, every single child can move forward, along this spectrum, towards a higher level of expertise, in any given area.

Why Should Any of Us Care?

We all want our children to grow up with hope, optimism and happiness. However, nurturing children's talents also contributes to national welfare. Talent development programmes have been commonplace in the United

States for many years. In 1972, the US Congress issued a report, which included the following, stating that the Nation's greatest resource for solving critical national problems in areas of national concern was its gifted and talented children and assert:[1]

> *Unless the special abilities of gifted and talented children are developed during their elementary and secondary school years, their special potential for assisting the Nation may be lost.*
>
> *– United States Congress 1972 (P.L. 95–561, Title IX, Part A, Section 901).[1]*

Can Parents Really Help?

Parents can help their children achieve highly. This is true across all social classes and ethnic groups – so no matter whether you are employed in a professional capacity or if you are unemployed, you, the parent, can make a difference – in fact, a big difference. This is explained in a study that Professor Charles Desforges and Alberto Abouchaar undertook for the UK Department of Education, in 2003.[2] Their report highlighted that parental involvement has the greatest impact during the early years and that the benefit of parental involvement among primary school children is greater than the quality of an individual school. Additionally, the authors found that the scale of this impact existed, irrespective of social class and ethnic group. Parents have a very important role to play in spotting their child's particular gifts, talents or special strengths. Our aim in writing this book is to support all parents who want to discover their child's gifts and talents and find opportunities for their children to help them build fulfilling and successful lives. It is also important to appreciate that all gifts and talents are precious and that we need a wide variety to have a rich and diverse society.

As part of a research project a few years ago, Valsa returned to India, where she was born, and interviewed children aged 10. What struck her most was that no matter what their parents' level of education was or the jobs they did, the parents all had very high expectations for their children.

Sunil, age 10, in India

Sunil's parents were coconut pickers, which is a poorly paid manual job. When he was asked where he thought he would be in 10 years' time, he said he will be training to be an engineer, lawyer or a doctor. We then asked him how he made that decision, and he replied: 'I decided that, but my parents have told me right from the start, as long as I can remember – that the way to make a better life for yourself is to study and make something of your life.'

Similar answers were given by many of the other boys and girls who were interviewed. Their parents had set high expectations for them and the children responded with setting high aspirations and goals for themselves.

One of the messages we would like to emphasise in this book is that your children's gifts and talents do not depend on your status in life. We have worked with many children from poor families. As described earlier in the 'Preface', Valsa participated in a BBC Television programme *Too Clever By Half*, which told the story of 6-year-old Ahmed. Ahmed showed multiple talents in mathematics, creative writing and science. His father was a road sweeper and the family lived in a council flat. However, Ahmed's mother played a crucial role in developing his potential. She talked to him, worked with him and encouraged him. Remarkably, she was not aware of how bright Ahmed was and she even said, 'I don't mind how clever he is or what his IQ is.' Impressively, she intuitively struck the right balance between encouraging Ahmed without putting any pressure on him.

We hope you enjoy joining us in undertaking a journey to find out more about aspects of giftedness, how it is defined by experts and how we may interpret the term from a practical point of view. We provide you with anonymised case histories of children and parents we know, as well as give you ideas on how parents can play a pivotal role in both identifying and realising their children's gifts and talents.

Structure of this Book

This book is divided into three parts and includes nine chapters.

Part I: Nurturing Children's Gifts

In *Chapter 1*, we provide you with a list of 10 factors to be aware of and which will help you find your child's special abilities and to turn their potential into success. In *Chapter 2*, we discuss the different viewpoints of ability and briefly trace how 'gifted education' developed over the years, including the history and details of the Gifted and Talented policy in England. Terms such as Intelligence Quotient (IQ), Multiple Intelligences and Emotional Intelligence are explained and demystified. We then go on, in *Chapter 3*, to discuss the all-important question: How do we identify our children's special gifts and talents? The challenges facing parents in spotting their children's special aptitudes are discussed with the support of research and case histories of children we have worked with. In *Chapters 4* and *5*, we provide practical ideas of how to turn children's special gifts into high achievement. We discuss the role of curiosity, imagination and creativity and how to ask high-quality questions that elicit high-quality responses. Among the different strategies we recommend are: encouraging children to think critically, talking, learning together at home and the importance of working together with your child's school.

Part II: Health and Wellbeing

Chapters 6 and *7* focus on the significant role of positive mental wellbeing in fulfilling children's potential. These chapters consider a number of different elements that contribute to healthier and happier lives, and discuss how you can help to develop your child's strength of character, reduce stress and anxiety and help them to become optimistic, resilient and happier. *Chapter 8* considers how you can help your child stay healthy and optimise their learning potential, by eating well and being physically active.

Part III: Conclusions

Finally, *Chapter 9* is the concluding section and summarises the answers to the 12 questions posed earlier in the *Parent Conversations* section.

The references (sources) we use in the different chapters are provided in the order of their appearance. Some of the important references are therefore referenced several times within a chapter.

Part I: Nurturing Children's Gifts

Chapter 1

TEN FACTORS TO HELP YOUR CHILD TOWARDS SUCCESS

Valsa Koshy and Elizabeth Koshy

● ●

In this book, we share with you our experiences of working with children, teachers, parents and carers. Much of the content in this book is based on over 20 years of work at Brunel University and the research Valsa has carried out on different aspects of what is usually described as *giftedness* and how it is developed. Many of the children we refer to in this book have been described as gifted, or talented or gifted and talented by their schools, voluntary organisations and the media. Their backgrounds are all different and their ages range from 4 to 16 years. We have had many communications from parents and one recurring question we have often been asked is, when were we going to write a book explaining what *giftedness* is and how parents can spot their children's gifts or talents and how to help develop them. Some of the parents told us, politely, but bluntly, that they had tried to read the academic papers and books Valsa has published and did not find them accessible in practical terms. Three of the most frequently asked questions by parents have been:

1. Is my child gifted?

2. How can I help my child, I think she/he has something special?

3. People from our backgrounds don't have clever children, how can our children ever become gifted?

As we explain later in the book (Chapter 2), there is no universally accepted definition for the commonly used term, *giftedness*. Quite often, when the word giftedness is used about people, it is to describe some of their special qualities or achievements. You read in the newspaper about gifted children who passed the General Certificate in Secondary Education (GCSE) or Advanced Level (A-Level) examinations by the age of 7 or 8 years (mainly in mathematics, you may have noticed) or you see television programmes about children who are able to calculate numbers quickly and memorise facts. These are, of course, achievements that are remarkable, but only part of the story. How frequently do we hear or read about what happens to these children and about their life course and longer-term trajectory?

According to the National Association for Gifted Children (NAGC) in the United States of America, gifted education has evolved over many decades.[1] One of the earliest recorded studies carried out was by Lewis Terman, who is often described as the father of the gifted education movement. The study was published with Stanford-Binet. It introduced the idea of intelligence testing and changed the face of American education. In 1921, Lewis Terman began the longest running longitudinal study of gifted children with an original sample of 1500 gifted children.[2] Terman published his book *Genetic Studies of Genius*, which described gifted children as different in several aspects. In the USA, the NAGC defines *'gifted individuals'* as those *'who demonstrate outstanding levels of aptitude (defined as an exceptional ability to reason and learn) or competence (documented performance or achievement in top 10% or rarer) in one or more domains'*.[1] These domains include any structured area of activity (e.g. mathematics, music, language) and/or set of sensorimotor skills (including painting, dance and sports).

In England, the definition is centred around students with high intellectual ability that are seen by teachers and others in the educational environment to be capable of advanced work. In 1999, for the first time in England, the Department for Education and Employment (DfEE) launched a policy document requiring schools to identify their most able students.[3] Later, in 2008, the Department provided a statement to describe the difference between gifted and talented students.[4] In the document, gifted students are described as those who excel academically in one or more subjects, such as history, science and maths, while talented students are those with the ability to excel in practical-based activities such as sport, music, dance and art. Additionally, schools in England use a range of terms including, able, more able, higher ability and high potential. The policy, which was launched in 1999, no longer exists and schools do not use a nationally accepted definition for giftedness in England.

Since Terman's work, there have been many changes in people's ideas about which children are gifted and what we mean by giftedness. Professor Robert Sternberg, an international expert on giftedness, has written a fascinating book, *Giftedness and Talent in the 21st Century* (2016).[5] He explains how we need to redefine giftedness to go beyond IQ tests; furthermore, that we need to consider how we identify and develop people who can make a contribution to make the world a better place. We agree with Sternberg that we cannot make the world a better place by labelling some children as gifted and thus creating a group of non-gifted children.

In this chapter, we outline 10 factors you should be aware of to be able to help spot and fulfil your children's special gifts and talents. Whatever your children's abilities are, these special strengths need nurturing and developing. In the later chapters of the book, we provide more detailed descriptions of what the labels 'gifted' and 'talented' mean in different contexts and also how these terms are defined by international experts in the field. We tell you in greater depth how to spot your children's unique abilities and strengths and how you can help them to reach their full potential.

Throughout the book, we provide examples of children we have worked with and people we know and we try to explain how you can transform your children's lives; the effort you make will be rewarding for both your children and you. We have changed many of the names of parents and children. We have promised them that our conversations will remain anonymous, as we have ensured in all our research and publications. This is due to ethical reasons and respect for others' privacy. What we write here is based on our research and experience, but many experts, nationally and internationally, have influenced our thinking and directions. They are acknowledged throughout the book.

The parents who approach us for help and guidance come from different backgrounds. Some are from lower income backgrounds, while others are professional parents who hold high-flying jobs and high salaries. Before we start outlining the 10 factors, we would like to share with you two communications we received from parents of different backgrounds we have met.

Case History: Father of Mia (4 years old)

Mia's father told us about his daughter:

When she started reading shop signs and words on shopping packages, we thought she was picking these up from our conversations. But when she started reading at three, it was a shock because I can't read that much and we are very poor. My wife can read but she hasn't taught Mia to read. You just don't expect this from our sort of background. We would like her to do well in life, but don't know how to help her.

With guidance and support, Mia's parents nurtured her love for reading. Mia's favourite place became the local library. She borrowed books and spent hours reading them. They bought books from local charity shops. When her teacher was told about her passion for reading, help also came from the school. Mia chose books from the school's library. Alongside her reading she started writing stories. Many of the stories found a space on the classroom display boards. An interesting observation from Mia's teacher was that her real gift was in reading and writing. Her writing abilities were well above that of her classmates and she was 'doing just fine' in other subjects. Mia's parents wanted to know if a child who is gifted in reading and writing should also be gifted in all subjects. We will be dealing with this later in the book.

Case History: Mother of Daniel (7 years old)

During a school visit, Daniel's mother told Valsa that she thought he must be bright as both she and her husband had attended prestigious schools and universities. However, Daniel was bored and often misbehaved. She thought he must be gifted and wondered how she could make him interested in learning.

Daniel's teacher, who was at that time working with Valsa on a government project, had chosen a new strategy to nurture and develop children's special abilities and interests.[6] As part of the project, Valsa had asked all the parents, teachers and children independently to write down what their children's special passions were. Interestingly, most teachers and children identified the same interests; but only 12 out of 30 parents had noticed any special interests of their children. Daniel's parents were among the 18 who had not. As part of the project, Daniel's mother asked her son: *'If you could choose to do one particular thing what would that be?'* Daniel's interest in shells was discovered. Books on shells were bought and internet sites explored. Daniel's teacher observed that acknowledging his new interest changed his attitude to learning and his written and oral work improved. With the help of an IT support teacher, Daniel prepared a presentation on shells to the class and the school assembly. A range of information was researched, which included the possible relationship between the depth of oceans and where different shells were found. Daniel's special interest was identified and it transformed his school life and that of his parents. One day Daniel's mother brought Valsa a rose flower and said, 'Thank you for everything. I can't get Daniel to even have his tea on time, it is shells, shells and more shells all the time.'

⭐ Based on over 20 years of experience, the most important message we have for parents is that instead of asking: Is my child gifted? ask, What is my child's special gift?

Find out that special interest or gift and nurture and develop it. If you follow this advice, you will find that your child works at that gift and all other aspects of his or her life should improve too. A child typically becomes happier and more fulfilled and may achieve higher grades. As our own research developed, we have come to know that separating children as gifted and not gifted is not a fruitful route to follow, as we will discuss later. In fact, we have never known any child who is an all-round *gifted* child in all school subjects: mathematics, writing, art, music and sport. Children excel and can often reach 'expert level' in specific areas while they may do 'very well' in other subjects too.

Case History: A Teacher's Perspective

After a workshop, where Valsa spoke about this belief, one teacher told her this:

You have made my day. I always thought that it is not possible to simply label a child gifted because she or he cannot really be gifted in every area. It is much better to specifically identify children's special gifts and make that a starting point for extending their involvement and enjoyment in other areas. When we were expected to select gifted children, for our gifted and talented group list in the school, I found it difficult to do, because quite often the exceptional artist and the sports expert were the ones who were left out by many of my colleagues who just looked at their test scores in Mathematics and English.

We wonder if our outstanding sporting heroes, like Sarah Storey, Mo Farrah, Laura Kenny, Ellie Simmonds, David Beckham, or Bradley Wiggins, would have been included in the gifted and talented (G&T) groups in their schools? They demonstrate genius level in their chosen field and possess tenacity not to be crushed by challenges they had to face. Would Richard Branson's entrepreneurial gifts have qualified him to be on the G&T list? He left school without taking his final exams and set up a magazine from which followed his worldwide success. Interestingly, many bright teenagers we have worked with think of Richard Branson as a role model to follow, because they admire his genial personality, his positive attitude towards his employees and even his infectious smile!

In the following sections, we provide you with ideas which parents have found useful in steering their children towards higher self-esteem and success.

Ten Factors to Help Turn Your Child's Potential into Success

We have developed the following 10 factors to impart knowledge and help you turn your child's potential into success. We discuss each of these in more detail in the subsequent chapters and provide you with practical plans for action.

(1) Your Child's Abilities do not Depend on Your Social Background

Your children can have very special strengths and abilities, irrespective of how rich or poor or educated you are. In many cases, we have found that children living in challenging circumstances who have been identified as having special gifts have achieved high levels of success with the right support and parents' access to information. A safe and nurturing environment and the right kind of parental support are key for all children to flourish. Much of our work has been focussed on the pursuit of what we describe as *submerged talent*, which may often be hidden and needs to be unlocked.[7]

An overwhelming desire to help children, like Mia, who we mentioned earlier, has contributed to the idea of this book. There is an ongoing public debate about the lack of social mobility in the UK. Children born to parents on low incomes or who have not been to university have a lower chance of obtaining a good education and entering well-respected and well-paid jobs than children with affluent parents, with good support systems and connections. In our research, we found that most parents have high aspirations for their children, what they lack is the confidence and knowledge regarding how to help them achieve these goals. Some of the intervention programmes we organised for teenagers from families living in challenging circumstances have been very successful. However, there is also a real need for interventions for younger children (5–10 years) from disadvantaged backgrounds. Some families do not have any books at home and live in relative poverty, and many children are hungry when they arrive at school and are given breakfast by schools first thing in the morning. Quite often, by the time these children leave primary school, there is a wide gap between their achievement and the average for their age group.

The Urban Scholars Programme (USP), which Valsa and her colleagues founded at Brunel University in 2000, was specially designed for 12–16 year olds who had the potential to succeed in life, but whose talents were hidden or submerged because of their external circumstances. Many were under-achieving and their test results were low. But, we were looking for their potential to do well and achieve, and a street-wise wisdom and ability to cope with and solve the challenges of everyday life. Participating inner-city schools worked with parents to nominate students for the programme. More than 1000 students from all over London have attended the 2–4-year programme. Students sometimes needed to make journeys across London to attend the programme on Saturdays once a month. Many of the students had to be gently coerced by their parents to wake up on a Saturday morning to travel to Brunel University.

Initiatives such as the USP are available in different forms in all British universities as part of the government's Widening Participation and social mobility initiatives. Parents told us that being selected for a university programme at the age of 12, itself, positively influenced many children's life courses.

Case History: Leon and his Mother

Leon's mother explained to us that no one in their family had ever been to university. Being selected to attend the USP motivated Leon and his sisters to aim for university. His sisters were impressed and excited by what he told them. Leon's mother felt that her family's lives changed as a result.

During an interview, Leon made the following comments about who influenced him:

I admire my mum most because of her will to do the impossible. She will do whatever she can for her children whether it is financial or emotional. She has always supported me in my education through the good and bad, although she says she doesn't know much about the education system.

Case History: Joey

A similar story was told by Joey:

People go on about our school being in a slum area, nobody going anywhere, but to be chosen for something like going to Brunel University at 12 was inspirational.

Case History: Anthony

We entered Anthony, another 12 year-old, for the World-Class Problem-Solving Tests.[8] They were designed by the UK's Qualifications and Curriculum Authority, in 2001, for the top 10% of students in the country. He passed the test and said:

I felt great and Professor Koshy told me the test was designed for the top 10% worldwide. I was really grateful to her for that opportunity. Even now it is acknowledged on my CV, in my Record of Achievement folder and I mentioned it at my university interview to study civil engineering.

(2) Intelligence is Not Fixed – You Can Change Your Child's Learning Potential

Being gifted has often been described as having a high Intelligence Quotient (IQ). Many regard an IQ score as a measure of a person's intelligence. One of the most memorable events Valsa recalls was telling groups of parents that we now have strong research evidence that tells us a person's intelligence is not fixed at birth and that it can increase with support. Some parents have commented that this was music to their ears! But let us now consider authoritative viewpoints from experts.

According to Linda Sheffield, a professor at Northern Kentucky University in the USA, who we have worked with, intelligence and ability can change.[9] She challenges the view that intelligence is a fixed entity, which cannot be increased.

Sheffield also explains another useful point. She talks about *'brain plasticity, the capacity of the brain to change with any type of learning'*. She asserts that the human brain maintains an amazing plasticity throughout life. With appropriate enrichment the brain *'never stops changing and adjusting – developing and pruning connections, organising and reorganising in response to experiences, even growing new neurons'*.[9]

The view that people can become more intelligent is also supported by other researchers, including the world-renowned expert, Carol Dweck, a social psychologist and professor at Stanford University, in the USA. She talks about developing a growth mindset in children.[10] A growth mindset is based on the belief that intelligence is a potential that can be developed and is not fixed. In the past few years, the style of teaching and feedback to children of many teachers has been influenced by the research and the writings of Carol Dweck. She has powerfully articulated the power of children's mindset on their achievement and success, regardless of whether they have been identified as gifted. Dweck describes the kind of habits parents and teachers can adopt to create a growth mindset. We will cover more on this later in the book.

A recent project funded by the Mayor of London and the Department for Education, in England, which Valsa led, involved introducing more classroom talk in mathematics lessons for children aged 6–7 years to enhance their achievement.[11] Valsa shared with teachers the ideas of Robin Alexander (2008)[12] about the power of talk in increasing children's learning abilities:

'Talk is necessary not just for learning, but also for the building of the brain itself as a physical organism, thereby expanding its power.'[12]

Alexander adds that the first years of life – and *'the primary phase of schooling, more or less – are years in which the brain in effect restructures itself (building cells, making new fibre connections between cells and pruning old ones), developing the capacity for learning, memory, emotional response and language are on a scale which decreases markedly thereafter. So, talking actively and vigorously fuels these processes'*.

The schools-based project was a success in terms of raising children's achievement. Talking is easy for parents to introduce too. We discuss this in more detail in later chapters.

A question that is quite often asked is:

> Where does intelligence originate from? Is it genetically inherited or environmentally developed?

Recent research suggests that it is a combination of both nature and nurture. However, one thing is certain, any genetically inherited intelligence can go to waste if it is not developed.

Many people believe that high IQ automatically equates to a very successful life course, but this is not necessarily the case.

Case History: Andrew, 34 years old

A few years ago, Valsa was in a coffee shop reading Howard Gardner's book *Intelligence Reframed*, when a young man, Andrew, approached her about the book.[13] Howard Gardner is an eminent Harvard University psychologist.[14,15] Andrew told Valsa that his IQ was tested when he was 12 years old and that his IQ score was 158, which puts him in the top 0.1% of the population. However, Andrew lived at home with his parents and thought it was the fault of his parents, his school and the government that he did not have a big job. Valsa quoted from Howard Gardner's book that, *'it's not how smart you are that matters, what really counts is how you are smart.'* As Valsa was interested in what happens to children with high IQ later in life, she met Andrew several times. It turned out that Andrew was interested in philosophy. His discussions with Valsa motivated him to study philosophy at university. He obtained a first class degree and now teaches at a further education college.

There are many more case histories like Andrew's in the world and that is why it is essential to find and channel your child's gifts and talents and develop and nurture them to fruition as early as possible.

(3) Instead of asking: 'Is my child gifted?' ask, 'What is my child's gift?'

Professor Joyce van Tassel-Baska (2005), an expert in gifted education, from the USA has contributed to both identifying giftedness and nurturing it, which has influenced educationists all over the world.[16] Tassel-Baska argues that a person is likely to show giftedness in specific and specialised fields. In one of her books, she cites Nobel laureates who are recognised for a single contribution. For example, Watson and Crick were awarded a Nobel prize for their contribution towards identifying the human DNA code. Van Tassel-Baska defines giftedness as a manifestation of general intelligence in a specific domain of human functioning at a level significantly above the norm, such as to show promise for original contributions to a field of endeavour. It is more practical and wiser to consider giftedness as a special ability in specific areas, whether it is mathematical, musical, social or artistic. In his award-winning book, *Frames of Mind*, Howard Gardner provided the world with a welcome and practical way of viewing intelligence and ability.[14] Gardner defines ability as being specific in some areas and introduces new ways of identifying special attributes, which also includes leadership skills and social skills as areas of giftedness and talent. His first list of seven types of intelligences is discussed in detail in Chapters 2 and 3. We also outline a list of different attributes you can observe to spot your child's special abilities. When Valsa lectures to teachers on Gardner's theory of *Multiple Intelligences*, they are often excited and begin to look at their students' abilities differently and report them in more positive terms, focussing more on strengths rather than weaknesses. It is time, we believe, that parents also consider the use of such frameworks to apply to their own children to spot and develop their strengths.

(4) Effort is Key

Most parents we talk to believe that a person's success depends on their cleverness, which some believe can be measured through an IQ test.

Here is something for you to think about. Time and time again we read about people who have achieved outstanding expertise and who worked very hard for their accomplishments. If you have watched the Channel 4 television programme *Child Genius*, you will see that almost every contestant for the title put in hours of study and practice. Another remarkable factor is the considerable amount of parental support the contestants receive.

We do need to take note of the role of effort. Experts such as Howe (1999)[17] and Ericsson (1996),[18] who have studied the role of effort, propose that the amount of time and practice a person spends on their specific ability is crucial if they want to reach world-class performance. Look at Olympic competitors, who typically organise their entire lives around training for several hours every day, in the hope of winning a medal in a competition that only takes place once every four years.

We also know that there are many examples of people who achieved great things, who had not shown extraordinary abilities when they were young. People like Albert Einstein were not described as highly gifted children; but they had a passion for learning and put in tremendous effort, which led to their great achievements. You will read more about this in Chapter 3.

After studying 120 outstanding achievers, including musicians, Olympians, mathematicians and scientists, the well-known educational psychologist, Benjamin Bloom (1985), concluded that, as children, most of them were not especially outstanding in their chosen field – before they started training.[19] Importantly, their parents played a crucial role in both identifying and developing their special abilities.

(5) Develop a Passion

We have always encouraged younger and older children who attend enrichment programmes at Brunel University to develop their interests and think about what they are passionate about. We have known 5–6 year olds who were passionate about stamp collections and butterflies, and 12–13 year olds developing interests in careers, which they wished to pursue, politics or, in some cases 'how to make millions of pounds!'

We met Richard Farleigh, a highly successful businessman and a former Dragon in the BBC TV programme *Dragons' Den*. Richard was one of 11 children born into a poor family who lived in a tent in the Australian outback. He recalls how his father was a violent alcoholic. Richard was taken into the foster care system and did not have any money or support when he re-emerged from it. However, he won a scholarship to study economics and mathematics at university, which, he says, changed his life and opened up opportunities for a successful career in global finance.

Interestingly, Richard Farleigh did not perform well in school and was assessed as *'a backward child with learning difficulties'*. However, Richard was a passionate chess player and one of the turning points in his educational life was when his intellectual ability was noted through his chess-playing. This recognition and encouragement helped to raise his self-confidence and levels of aspiration, which subsequently led to a university scholarship, a first class degree, a fruitful career and total financial independence.

What struck us most during our meeting with Richard was his sharp mind, humility and appreciation of the role of hard work. His story also highlighted that it is possible to be very successful in life, despite adverse circumstances in childhood. His grit and determination ultimately overturned his disadvantage.

Many famous and successful people we have heard of – the author J.K. Rowling and the physicist Einstein – had strong interests and pursued them for many years before becoming high achievers in their fields.

Let your children tell you or show you what their passions are, encourage their curiosity and work with them. Remember Daniel, whose passion for shells influenced his love for learning and to higher achievement later in life. Start a 'passion project' (as children often describe it to us) with your children. With the internet and the rich resources available to us these days, possibilities are limitless.

(6) Start Early

A research paper Valsa published with Professor Nancy Robinson, a psychologist and expert in Early Years from the University of Washington (2006), highlighted that most successful adults who excelled in their areas of expertise had supportive parents or mentors when they were young.[20]

We know that it is important to try to spot children's special interests and abilities from an early age. Again, according to Howard Gardner (1983), [14] it should be possible to identify an individual's intellectual profile (proclivities) at an early age and then draw upon that knowledge to enhance that person's educational opportunities and options.

Adele Adkins is an internationally successful singer and song-writer, who many view has made an outstanding contribution to popular music. Adele was born in Tottenham, London. She was raised by her mother from a young age; her mother, who loved music herself, exposed Adele to a range of music genres from a very young age. Adele has shared that she started to sing aged four and became fascinated by different voices. This early musical environment may have sparked her passion for singing and writing song lyrics.

So what do you do as parents? Find that particular interest, gift or talent as early as possible – the earlier the better. Of course children change their interests and passions, but that is fine. Your child may be interested in creative writing, mathematical puzzles, music, athletics, painting or show leadership qualities. A child we know showed outstanding ability in playing the commercial game *Four in a Row* and was able to place her counters in such a way that she nearly always won against adults. This alerted her parents to her having a possible strength in playing chess and her parents introduced her to chess, which proved fruitful.

We also know parents who pressurise their children in specific areas of their choice, which are often rejected by the children and lead to misbehaviour and turn them off learning altogether. There is also the inevitable pressure from schools, because of national curriculum tests and other hurdles that children need to jump. It is important to strike a balance and not push too hard. What about doing school homework? We have often advised parents to make a list of what they are going to do, including homework, and add the child's passion (e.g. drawing, making up plays or making models) to the list as a final treat. You will, hopefully, observe more cooperation and less negative attitudes. You may also notice children wanting to spend more time on their chosen item!

(7) Encouraging a Growth Mindset and Use of Praise and Feedback

As part of the research Valsa carried out, we found most teachers who took part in the research did not consider the use of the label 'gifted' useful in their classroom practice (Koshy, Pinheiro and Portman Smith, 2012).[21] Interestingly, a similar study we carried out in 1996 and presented at the American Educational Research Association conference had reached the same conclusion. The use of the label gifted was found to have negative effects on children in a number of ways. Although some children (and their parents) viewed being on a gifted and talented (G&T) register as a remarkable achievement, many others felt under pressure to live up to the label and in some cases had to endure teasing and even bullying.

As mentioned earlier, Carol Dweck believes that the concept of labelling children as being gifted can cultivate a fixed mindset within them. They may subsequently believe that their qualities are carved in stone and that creates an urgency to prove oneself over and over (Dweck, 2006).[10] Dweck encourages us to develop a growth mindset which is based on the belief that individuals can cultivate their own qualities and change through their own application, effort and experience. Dweck asserts that a person's true potential is unknown (and unknowable) – that it's impossible to foresee what can be accomplished with years of passion, toil and training.

However, praise can also be over-used. A 5-year-old girl we know enjoys mathematics and has a very good understanding of the concept of number, including large numbers. Her parents praised her for this; perhaps over-praised in that one day we noticed her reluctance to be engaged in writing, even rejecting it. When asked why she did not like writing, her response was 'you can't get so many ticks for writing. I like ticks'. What she meant must be that she was so used to obtaining correct answers for mathematics, which did not require further effort or improvement. Her parents told her that if she was good at maths, she could be good at writing as well, if she puts in more effort. It worked in that the reluctant writer started talking about constructing stories and plays. Her parents may have inadvertently overdone the praise and created a sense of failure when she had to approach an area that did not have instant success.

According to Dweck's work, praising children is very important, but we have to be careful of the nature of the praise and feedback we give. We must try to avoid giving children a false sense of security by only giving praise and positive feedback; try looking at their work and suggesting how they can improve it. It is also useful to give children the message that it is good enough but with more effort they might do better, or ask them if they can challenge themselves and think of a harder question.

Dweck (2006) also tells us that 'labelling' children as *'gifted'*, can lead them to think that they do not need to make effort and at the first hurdle or challenge they may give up.[10] Praising them as having high intelligence can often lead to them to be crushed at the smallest experience of failure.

(8) Fight Low Expectations and Create Optimism and Self-belief in your Children with Special Educational Needs and Disabilities (SEND)

The most rewarding work we have done and both felt extremely positive about has involved working with children who have special educational needs and disabilities (SEND). All children with SEND have gifts too – in academic and non-academic areas. We strongly believe that society needs gifts in every field to flourish and that all gifts are of equal importance. We are always saddened when we hear about low expectations and judgemental attitudes. All children deserve their gifts to be acknowledged and nurtured. Some examples of children we have encountered come to mind.

Case History: Jack, 9 years old

We met a mother, Claire, whose son has severe learning difficulties and struggled for years with 'other parents' judgemental attitudes'. However, Claire shared with us how incredibly loving her son is and what substantial emotional intelligence he possesses, with tremendous ability to understand other people. She describes her son as 'the light of my life'. She also shared that she finds labels such as gifted and highly intelligent very depressing and elitist. She views every child as having a unique, special ability, which, in her son's case, is 'emotional intelligence' and she believes every child is 'differently-abled' or 'uniquely-abled'. We both really appreciated this viewpoint and totally agree with this perspective.

Case History: Sam, 10 years old

Another parent shared how, when his son, Sam, with Attention Deficit Disorder (ADD) became interested in drawing, he spent hours drawing buildings with tremendous detail and accuracy. The confidence this gave him filtered through to other school subjects and his performance in all subjects improved.

Case History: Zak and his grandmother

Donna told us about her grandson, Zak, who has severe visual impairment in one eye. Zak was recently accepted into one of the most prestigious schools in the UK after taking a competitive entrance examination. Zak is very bright and determined not to let his condition 'bring him down'. His determination together with his parents' support prevented what otherwise might have been a very difficult and different experience. Sadly, not every child with a disability is always that lucky.

Case History: Chloe, 5 years old

Chloe, who has a special educational need, was bullied by a child in her class. She was repeatedly called 'stupid'. To add to the sadness of the parents, her teacher told them that her maths was poor and the explanation given was that she didn't use counters to add numbers, but just worked them out in her head. Valsa knows this child and noticed her exceptional ability in working with number patterns at the age of 5; one example was when she mentally worked out the twentieth number in the series of triangular numbers. Her teacher may have had low expectations of her and if the parents did not persist and fight this perception, the talent of a mathematically talented child may have been lost.

We also know of many cases of children who have specific learning difficulties achieving the highest grades in school examinations or are very capable in non-academic subjects, although, sadly, some of the children we know have not been so fortunate and have been called 'stupid' or other cruel names. Parents need to be aware that a child's special educational need or disability does not prevent them from reaching high levels of expertise in their chosen field(s). High expectations of teachers, parents and the children themselves are often a prerequisite for high achievement.

Professor Montgomery has long been involved in addressing the challenge of identifying children's special gifts and talents if they had special needs – physical, or emotional or a specific learning difficulty.[22] Children who have one or more special educational needs or disabilities and who also have high ability are described as having *Dual or Multiple Exceptionality* (DME). These children are also sometimes referred to as 'twice exceptional'. Some examples of SEND include: dyslexia, Autistic Spectrum Disorder (ASD), Attention Deficit Hyperactivity Disorder (ADHD), developmental co-ordination difficulties, sensory issues, mobility and physical problems (including visual and hearing impairment) and certain medical conditions. It can sometimes be a challenge for teachers and parents to identify these children's gifts and to make appropriate provision for them. Parents need to encourage their children to find and pursue an interest, be optimistic, determined and success frequently follows. Furthermore, parents need to encourage their children to aim high and not lose self-esteem due to their SEND.

(9) Encourage Determination, Persistence and Optimism

We have always encouraged children attending our university programmes to practise perseverance and determination. Professor Martin Seligman, a renowned psychologist at the University of Pennsylvania, believes that optimism is something one can learn.[23] Valsa quoted Seligman in her book, *Teaching Young Gifted and Talented Children (4–7)* and the concept was very well received by readers.[24]

In all our work with children and parents, we found that children who had high aspirations were more optimistic about their future. When we interviewed the children's parents we also noticed that the parents of the more optimistic children were more hopeful about their children's future and that they fostered this trait in them.

Case History: Sandra

Sandra was 12 years old when she joined Brunel University's Urban Scholars Programme (USP). She attended a south London school, where she said she did not expect to achieve the grades to obtain a place to study Medicine. Her parents – a bus driver and a beauty therapist – encouraged her to keep her dream alive and when she missed the grades to join a medical course, she applied to study for a degree in biomedical science at a medical school and was determined to transfer to study medicine. She quoted back to Valsa, what she usually tells the USP children, 'be determined, work hard and be persistent'.

In Paul Tough's book *How Children Succeed*, he enthusiastically endorses the power of character building in children for their success.[25] Tough gives many examples where children who succeeded against disadvantage were the ones who possessed gifts of optimism and resilience. His book is often seen as having the potential to improve children's future. Valsa was impressed by it enough to buy copies for all her colleagues and made them read it too.

The roles of persistence and optimism were very much a theme that we picked up for a project we undertook with parents from socially deprived areas. One mother of a 12-year-old told us:

> *I tell my boy that a black boy can do well. You don't have to be a statistic of black children failing in school or in life. Aspirations determine your altitude. Look at President Obama – he must have had high aspirations to reach the White House. Be positive – you have the gift to do well. I have seen that gift of determination in my son since he was 2 years old.*

Valsa shared with her students the remarkable qualities and determination of the competitors we witnessed in the Olympics and Paralympics in London, in 2012, and recently, in Rio de Janeiro, in 2016. Sporting success is evidence of the role of determination and grit.

(10) Take Care of Your Children's Mental and Physical Wellbeing

Professor Martin Seligman very elegantly echoes what most parents' aspirations for their children are. He believes that parents want their children to have *more than just 'healthy bodies'*.[23] Seligman (1995) suggests *'friendship and love, confidence, a sense of justice, courage and resilience (when faced by failures and setbacks) are all important too'*.[23]

In Chapters 6 and 7, we outline strategies that parents can use to support their children's mental wellbeing, which can, in turn, contribute to their personal happiness, self-confidence, long-term achievement and future success. Specifically, we discuss aspects relating to sleep, stress and anxiety, the effects of bullying, developing assertiveness and emotional resilience. In Chapter 8, aspects of physical wellbeing are introduced, including how parents can help to establish good eating habits and encourage physical activity in their children's lives, which can impact on their physical health, learning potential and overall wellbeing.

We hope that the 10 factors outlined above provide an initial set of points for you to reflect on. These factors are expanded on in the subsequent chapters of the book.

In the next chapter, we explain the viewpoints on giftedness, talent and high ability to provide you with a background. We also provide you with views from international experts, as well as our own experiences and perspectives.

Key Points

In this chapter, we outlined 10 factors for you to be aware of and consider to help your child to develop their gifts and potential:

1. Your child's abilities are not related to your social background.
2. Intelligence is not fixed – you can change your child's learning power.
3. Instead of asking: 'Is my child gifted?' ask, 'What is my child's gift?'
4. Effort is key in turning potential into high performance.
5. Develop your child's special passions and interests.
6. Start identifying and nurturing interests early.
7. Encourage a growth mindset.
8. Fight low expectations and create hope and self-belief in your children with special educational needs or disabilities.
9. Encourage determination, persistence and optimism.
10. Take care of your child's mental and physical wellbeing.

Chapter 2

VIEWS ON GIFTEDNESS, TALENT AND HIGH ABILITY

Valsa Koshy

What do We Mean by Giftedness, Talent and High Ability?

Many teachers and parents are puzzled by the question of how to identify a gifted or very able child. Before we can identify giftedness, we first have to be clear on what we mean by that term. The understanding of giftedness has changed significantly since the 1980s and approaches taken by different schools and governments have evolved over that time. One of the most influential researchers has been Professor Howard Gardner, at Harvard University, who developed his theory of Multiple Intelligences in his seminal work, *Frames of Mind* (1983).[1,2] Gardner proposes that people possess a range of different intelligences, which we discuss later in this chapter. In his book and the many publications that followed, he provides us with a practical way of identifying children's multiple talents, which, in turn, should help every parent to nurture and develop those talents.

Over the years, I have received hundreds of letters, e-mails and phone calls from parents asking if their child was gifted. These requests for help – for explanations of what giftedness, talent and high ability mean and how to spot them – are much higher in number after watching television programmes about gifted children, or reading newspaper articles about children entering examinations several years earlier than others of their age (which mostly seems to be in mathematics). To illustrate what I am trying to share with you we have used examples, throughout this book, drawn from parents' communications. Here are two stories of children that highlight the complexity of the concept of giftedness.

Case History: Stephen, 8 years old

One of the early entries in my ongoing diaries relates to 8-year-old Stephen who attended our Saturday classes. One lunchtime I was walking with the children to the refectory for lunch (the highlight of the children's day – being in a room with undergraduates where they felt important to be at a university).

Stephen asked me if I could keep a 'top secret' and I said I could. The conversation went like this:

Stephen: My Mum had my IQ tested and it is 144.

Valsa: That is good.

Stephen: That makes me severely gifted – that means I am very clever.

Valsa: Is there something special you do because of your cleverness?

Stephen: That is the sad thing. I have twilight lessons. I have a tutor who comes twice a week to teach me maths so that I can do GCSE maths exam next year.

Valsa: Do you enjoy it?

Stephen: Not really, I would like to watch animal programmes instead. I am really keen on animals and their habitats.

By the end of this conversation, we had reached the refectory and I had discovered that Stephen was very humorous, but not too happy with the extra lessons after school. This raised questions in my mind. Children aged 15–16 years usually take GCSE examinations. I knew Stephen's mother and found her very caring and wanting to do the very best for her son. I was curious as to why Stephen was being prepared to take the exam when he was 8 years old.

Case History: Matthew, 5 years old

A few years ago, the *Times Educational Supplement*, a weekly newspaper for teachers and others who are interested in education, printed an anecdote based on one of my experiences in a classroom.[3] I spoke to Matthew (5 years old) when he was sitting at his desk, not looking very happy.

The following conversation took place:

Valsa: So, tell me what you are doing

Matthew: Just waiting, waiting, waiting … (he paused) … as I always do. I am a waiter. I always have to wait until everyone else has finished. I have to do extra work, more than anyone else because I finish work quickly. I would like to build a rocket and try it and write a story about an adventure in space. Shall I tell you a story about me visiting space and talking to the people there?

The story Matthew relayed to me was very imaginative and drew on his extraordinary knowledge of aspects of space. The question it again raised for me was: is he gifted, and what are his *gifts*?

One point that struck me about Matthew is that although he was described as gifted by his school, he, like Stephen, was only performing at a high level in mathematics. His writing skills were not well developed. Judging from the conversations I had with him and listening to his humorous and imaginative narrations of events, I thought, with encouragement and support, he may become a very effective creative writer. Again, it raised important questions for me.

Can anyone be gifted in everything? Or are people gifted, talented or highly able in specific areas?

As Matthew's class teacher, Melissa, was a past teacher-trainee student of mine, I was happy to talk to her about this, hoping that she wouldn't think that I was judging her teaching, based on Matthew's exchange with me. Melissa told me that she was aware of Matthew's frustration in having to wait for others to finish, but had not had a chance to talk to him and explore what his real interests were. His real interest, she explained, was not mathematics, although she said that mathematics was the only subject the school had suitable resources to extend children.

I noted one important point from the above two case histories and other similar conversations; these young children had special interests, but these were not encouraged mainly because the parents and teachers had not either really discovered them or did not have the resources to explore them.

The idea of high ability, giftedness and talent is complex. As I alluded to earlier, there is no agreed definition for any of these terms. In my professional life, I have come across children with a range of gifts and talents who have varied interests and passions. I have worked with children who have scored highly in academic examinations, but not shown much interest in developing any other interests; I have also known children who have spent hours developing their special interests and have achieved outstanding levels of accomplishment, in particular fields or domains, whether it is in mathematics, poetry composition, sport or music. High ability, aptitude, giftedness or talent – whatever terminology we use – manifest themselves in so many forms which make it extremely difficult to have a single definition to describe these terms. An article in *The International Handbook of Giftedness and Talent* (Monks, Heller & Passow, 2000) explains the challenge that faces us all very clearly.[4] The authors state that the *'basic problem in building a theory about giftedness is that it is a multi-faceted phenomenon'*. They ask whether a single theory can account for the occurrence of 4-year-olds who play chess like adults, young children who are concert-class performers or who perform exceptionally well on academic tasks or school-age children who develop patentable inventions? Further, the authors ask *'if a single theory can explain the rare Einsteins, Shakespeares, Nijinskys and similar talented individuals, as well as a child whose 'giftedness' appears to be achieving unusually well academically, as measured by standardised achievement tests?'*[4]

Again, note the people listed in this quote. They excelled in specific areas. Were they born with a gift in these areas or had they developed their talent and expertise over the years? I will discuss this more later.

In spite of the difficulties in arriving at precise definitions of terms, there is common agreement among many educationists and parents, that children have special abilities, which require nurturing and developing.

Gifted and Talented, or Gifts and Talents?

The complexity in understanding the concept of high ability may explain why the use of the terms 'gifted' and 'talented' and the process of labelling children as such continues to pose a big problem among teachers in the UK and overseas. The range of social, economic and political perspectives may possibly mean that a unified definition could never materialise.

Let us try to demystify these words to acquire a better understanding of children's abilities and what may be possible. Based on the research projects I have carried out at Brunel University and drawing on experts in the field of talent development, I will explain the terms I use and what they actually mean.

What I am about to say should make you feel more optimistic about your child's education and wellbeing.

> ⭐ Instead of asking: *'Is my child gifted?'* we should ask, *'What is my child's gift?'*

In the subsequent chapters, I discuss how you can spot your child's special gifts or talents and how to develop them. With increased self-esteem and being encouraged to develop what they enjoy, excel in and where they may achieve higher levels of accomplishment, children often display more interest in learning in other areas too.

In the field of gifted education, the question of terminology has always been under constant revision. In the 1950s, the term gifted was used on the basis of the results of Intelligent Quotient (IQ) tests, initially carried out by Terman (1925) for the purpose of selecting pupils for specially designed educational programmes.[5] Terman used an IQ score of 140 as a cut-off point for selection, although some exceptions were made for pupils with scores of 135–139 (Feldhusen, 2003).[6] In the past few decades, a broadening of the concept of ability has led to a revision of Terman's definition of giftedness based on IQ scores. I provide an overview of the IQ related perspective on ability later in this chapter.

How did 'Gifted' Education Develop Over the Years?

In this section, I provide an overview of how gifted education has developed and then go on to consider some of the views proposed by international experts on what constitutes giftedness, talent and high ability. I will also take a closer look at how gifted education has evolved and developed in the UK.

The first interest in giftedness can be traced back to the work of ancient philosophers. George (1992) mentions Socrates and Plato as two historic figures who defined giftedness as the ability to move more quickly through levels of knowledge and to achieve a deeper understanding of this knowledge.[7] Early definitions of ability were based on a measure of Intelligence Quotient (IQ) described as the 'general intelligence factor' (the g factor), indicating pupils' ability to reason and make connections. Tests similar to IQ tests are sometimes used for selection purposes in some schools in the form of entrance examinations. Psychologists use IQ tests for diagnostic purposes; for example, to explore possible problems with learning or behaviour.

Although it is accepted that IQ tests do serve some useful purpose, their use as an exclusive means of identifying high ability or aptitudes is questioned by many. Critics point out that many factors can affect IQ test results. The way a child feels on the day of the test, or even the way the test is carried out can influence the final score. Cultural bias in the test questions may also affect children's performance in the test. In addition, a child who may be creative or is a divergent thinker may not do well in an IQ test. A few years ago, during a visit to a Centre for Gifted Education in the USA, where IQ-based tests were used, I was told that some children challenged the nature of the questions in the test itself and considered *more sensible* options and solutions (according to children) to the Multiple-Choice Questions. As a result, they obtained lower scores, although they were considered the brightest by their teachers.

Many educationists and psychologists believe that a single measure of intelligence does not acknowledge the diverse talents, aptitudes and abilities of pupils. They believe that a broader concept of giftedness and the assessment of a range of abilities are more likely to lead to an enhanced quality of practical provision for gifted children.

The Role of Gender

A US study of 400 children, recently published in *Science* (Bian *et al.*, 2017) found that at age 5, boys and girls thought their own gender was 'brilliant'.[8] However, just one year later, age 6 years, girls start to see themselves as less talented compared with boys (BBC News, 2017).[9] The research involved a number of experiments conducted by the team from Princeton University, New York University and the University of Illinois. One experiment involved the children listening to a story about someone who was 'really, really smart', but it was not clear from the story who this person related to. The children then had to guess who the character was from four pictures (two men and two women). At age 5, boys picked men and girls picked women about three-quarters (75%) of the time. However, worryingly, one year later, aged 6 years, boys were still picking men while girls were now slightly more likely to pick men too. The authors suggested media, teachers, parents and other children were influencing these findings. The study highlights stereotypes may be created at an early age. Therefore, we need to consciously help to raise and maintain girls' aspirations from a young age.

There is also a potential gender bias for Multiple Choice Questions (MCQ) examinations. While Elizabeth was at medical school, she had to complete *negatively marked* MCQ examinations, where a correct answer was awarded with a mark (+1), but a wrong answer resulted in a loss of a mark (−1). Evidence available at the time showed that female medical students were more cautious than their male counterparts and were less likely to risk guessing an answer for fear of the negative marks if they were wrong, whereas male medical students were less risk-averse and were more inclined to guess answers that they were not entirely sure about. As there is a reasonable probability of guessing the correct answer, the male students may have had better chances of scoring higher marks. The negative scoring was subsequently abandoned and the MCQ marks for female candidates improved!

Differing Views on Ability Among International Experts

Our own research and existing literature have revealed that there are various and opposing viewpoints about giftedness and talent. Some believe that a fixed percentage of a population, say 1 or 2%, can be identified as gifted and talented (G&T) individuals and they should be provided with special programmes. Others believe that we should focus on maximising opportunities for developing gifts and talents in *all* pupils by moving away from labelling a sub-group as gifted.

In his speech at one of our national conferences, Professor Joseph Renzulli, an international expert in gifted education, shared with us his belief that: 'A rising tide lifts all ships.'[10] Claxton and Meadows (2009) maintain that in education our job is to help children develop *'zeal and hard work'* that will enable them to emerge as *'gifted and talented in their unique ways'*.[11] Teachers who plan their lessons considering the high-achieving children in their class, raise both their own and the children's expectations, so children of all abilities benefit.

For a research project, which was designed to find out teachers' perceptions and views of giftedness and the concept of high ability, we explored four main themes (Koshy and Pinheiro-Torres, 2013).[12] The first of these is a conception many hold, based on the belief that giftedness is a single dimensional measure and can be assessed through tests, including IQ tests. In practice, this view involves teachers identifying gifted pupils using traditional tests. Renzulli (2005)[10] describes this view as *'school house giftedness'* and proposes a (second) *'broader'* perspective on giftedness. In his 'Three-Ring' model, Renzulli emphasises other indicators such as creativity, task-commitment and motivation, as equally important as the level of ability, for the fulfilment of giftedness.

We already mentioned Gardner's (1983, 1993)[1,2] ground breaking theory of Multiple Intelligences, which postulates that people may possess a range of different intelligences. van Tassel-Baska (2005), another US expert, holds the view that giftedness cannot be described as a single idea but that it is, in fact, multi-dimensional.[13] Sternberg (2000), a guru in proposing how to develop giftedness, suggests that giftedness is not a fixed state, but is *'developing expertise and is modifiable'*.[14]

Interestingly, some experts provide a third viewpoint. Borland (2005) argues that giftedness is a superfluous or out-dated concept and that it is a social invention that creates divisions in society that have no constructive purpose.[15]

A view of giftedness presented by Howe (1999)[16] and Ericsson (1996)[17] suggests that all children are born more or less equal regarding the specific abilities associated with any given domain of achievement and that, over time, children become differentiated according to the amount of domain-specific expertise they acquire. The amount of practice and the more time the person spends mastering domain-specific knowledge and skills, the closer he or she will be towards attaining world-class performance.

So, as you can see, there are many views and conceptions on ability and what it entails.

I believe that it is important for parents, teachers and all those who work with children to consider and review the different viewpoints that exist surrounding what these words mean. A careful consideration of each of these viewpoints of ability should help you form your own framework of understanding.

What is the Intelligence Quotient (IQ)?

As previously mentioned, when referring to giftedness and talent, it is quite common for people to talk about these terms in relation to high Intelligence Quotient (IQ) scores. IQ scores are results obtained in psychometric testing and they provide a single score as a measure of intelligence. There are several commonly used IQ tests, which are usually carried out by psychologists, to assess the level of ability. For most tests, a score of 100 denotes 'average' intelligence. The tests are all calibrated along a comparable scale. Using the Wechsler Intelligence Scales, an IQ score of 130 or above has conventionally been an indicator that someone is gifted. If a large sample of children (say, aged 10) in any country are tested you are likely to obtain a picture (bar chart) as shown in Figure 2.1. IQs of 150 and above are suggestive of exceptional potential to learn.

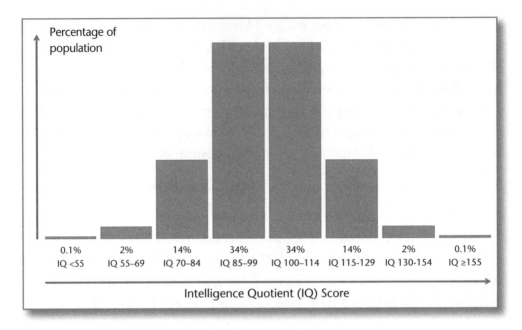

Figure 2.1: The approximate distribution of IQ levels among the population.

Support for IQ testing is based on the view that the population can be represented by a 'normal distribution curve', which can be approximated by a bar chart representation, as shown in Figure 2.1. It is symmetrical and perhaps easier to understand as a model for providing guidance about intelligence. The administration of IQ tests is recommended by some as the most accurate predictor of the potential for doing well academically. Others challenge the usefulness of attaching a number to a child, dismiss it as a pointless exercise and maintain that a high IQ does not offer any practical basis for educational strategy, neither does it predict higher ability in a particular discipline.

Potential Disadvantages of Defining and Labelling Children by IQ

There are some important reservations about labelling children as having a particular level of intelligence. Discovering that a child is above or below a threshold level of intelligence can, critics believe, potentially have undesirable and unintended consequences.

Case History: Anna, 7 years old

Anna's parents believed that their daughter was very bright and they arranged an IQ test. However, her mother, Claire, was bitterly disappointed when the test resulted in an IQ score of 126. Claire phoned me and explained that if Anna's score was 130 or more, she would have been classified as gifted, and that she could no longer ask Anna's school for special provision. I prompted Claire to consider that Anna was still just as bright and capable as she had been the day before. I urged Claire to encourage Anna to talk about her special interests, and to discuss together what they could do. I also suggested telling Anna's teachers about her special passions, so that they too could provide her with opportunities to explore and develop these interests.

It emerged that Anna knew a lot about birds and had wanted to write a series of books on birds for young children. In consultation with her teacher, we encouraged her to undertake a project to write a book about birds, and to use a computer package for the presentation. Anna did more than that. With the help of her parents, she took photographs of birds and included colour photos in her book, and the bound book was displayed in the school hall. Anna's subsequent books covered a range of aspects of bird life, such as migration and distances covered by birds, eating habits and other areas. Her general attitude to school changed and she was no longer 'bored', as her mother put it. Both the parents and the teachers were thrilled with the outcome. Anna's story had a very positive outcome, and she later studied for a science degree. Anna grew in confidence through dedication, hard work and perseverance. Most importantly, Anna also had a happy childhood!

This example of testing for IQ highlights the possible drawbacks of relying only on tests to classify children as gifted or not gifted. Do a few marks or scores matter anyway? In Anna's case, if she had obtained four more IQ points that would not have helped her teachers to provide for her differently, or change her as a person or her life course. The high-quality provision that Anna received in this case was not based on a measured test result, but on communicating with her and finding out what her particular interests were.

Anna is an example of a child who did not receive the desired label based on IQ testing. You may also recall the story of 34-year-old Andrew from Chapter 1. Andrew had been given the information that his IQ was 158 as a child, but he struggled to translate that into concrete outcomes in his life. So, simply being told a child has a high IQ, does not equate to automatic success and happiness in life.

Hence our take-home message is: **there can be potential for problems whether a child passes the predefined IQ threshold or not**.

History of Gifted and Talented (G&T) Education in England

For the readers in England and others who may be interested in the history of how gifted and talented (G&T) education has evolved within UK policy, here is a brief summary of the development of G&T education in England. Scotland and Wales have their own framework of provision for high ability students. Concerns about the lack of provision for higher ability children had been highlighted for at least three decades by Her Majesty's Inspectorate in England (HMI, 1978; 1979).[18,19] In 1992, HMI pointed out that the needs of the 'very able' were not being met in many schools and that such pupils were not sufficiently challenged.[20] This was followed by a speech, by a senior HMI official, McIntosh (1994)[21] at a national conference on gifted education, who called for action:

> *There is very clear evidence that focusing sharply on what the most able can achieve raises the expectations generally, because essentially it involved consideration of the organisation and management of teaching and learning.*[21]

The Labour Government, following the general election, in 1997, introduced the G&T education policy for schools in England (DfEE, 1999).[22]

Schools were required to:

- identify 5–10% of their most able pupils as G&T and place them on a register (the percentage refers to each school's population);
- implement a distinct teaching and learning programme for G&T pupils.

Government funding was granted for each local authority in England to appoint staff with responsibility for G&T education. All schools were encouraged to nominate a member of staff to implement the policy in their school and many schools created the role of a G&T co-ordinator. Schools were expected to identify and maintain a register of their G&T pupil population (top 10%) and to make appropriate provision for them. So, formal attention was now being paid to developing children's talents.

As mentioned in Chapter 1, the Department for Children, Schools and Families (2008) provided specific guidance for schools.[23]

The formal DfES definition for G&T was provided, as follows:

Gifted: the top 5–10% of pupils per school as measured by actual or potential achievement in English, Maths, Science, History, Geography, Modern Foreign Languages, RE, ICT or Design and Technology.

Talented: the top 5–10% of pupils per school as measured by actual or potential achievement in the subjects of Art, Music, PE or the Performing Arts.

It may sound a simple process to identify these children, but there were inevitably problems. For example, in our research (Koshy and Pinheiro-Torres, 2013), it was found that many teachers felt uneasy about labelling children as gifted and that they preferred to use the term 'more able' to describe these pupils.[24] Another problematic area for teachers was the separation of G&T students. The government definition of the phrase 'Gifted and Talented' – clustering the two terms, gifted and talented – was seen to be confusing. Most schools did not have separate registers for G&T students and it raised several questions about how students were identified and placed on the register. One question asked by teachers, which we were also debating among ourselves, was whether students who are good in academic areas, such as mathematics and English, also had to be good at creative or physical subjects to be included in the G&T register? Was it likely that children who displayed very high abilities in the creative and physical areas may be missed altogether from the register?

Discussions at a Commons Select Committee hearing, to review progress in G&T education, was conducted with key players in early February 2010 (House of Commons, 2010)[25] and focussed on the 'inconsistency' of the policy and the impact in classrooms, generally, with regard to provision being 'patchy' (Evans, 2010)[26].The Select Committee concluded that the best course of action was to allow schools to manage their own implementation of the G&T policy.

Howard Gardner's Theory of Multiple Intelligences

Case History: A Lecture Theatre of Teacher Trainees

I started a session by asking a lecture theatre full of teacher trainees:

Valsa: Put your hands up if you are gifted.

Audience of teacher trainees: (Three hands went up out of 160 students in the lecture hall.)

Valsa: Oh dear. (I said and smiled.)

Valsa: (Then I asked.) *Put your hands up if you are gifted or especially talented in something.*

Audience: (More than half the audience put their hands up.)

Valsa: Why did you put your hands up for this question and not for the first one?

We subsequently spent quite some time listening to students passionately talking about what they were very talented in – art, music, mathematics, tennis and creative writing. I asked them what this meant in the context of them teaching children.

Teachers often struggle with the idea of labelling a child as gifted. Most children are likely to have specific abilities in some fields and may not show all-round ability. A highly gifted child in creative writing may not exhibit high performance or aptitude in other subject areas, such as history, music or sport.

Following the publication of the Marland Report (1972) there has been a shift in thinking in the USA from measurement of general abilities to specific abilities.[27]

The report proposed six categories of G&T children in the following areas:

1. general intellectual ability

2. specific academic aptitude

3. creative or productive thinking

4. leadership ability

5. visual or performing arts

6. psychomotor ability

Howard Gardner's Theory of Multiple Intelligences (MI) won international recognition, and overwhelming acceptance by the education community because of the way he persuades many that ability shows itself in a variety of ways, and that children possess different talents which need to be recognised (1983, 1993)[1,2].

Since the MI theory was launched, many educational programmes around the world have been based on Gardner's views. The Theory of Multiple Intelligences describes ability in domain-specific terms. On the basis of his work with prodigies and those with partial brain damage, Gardner proposed seven intelligences, acknowledging that there are more. Other Intelligences – naturalist and existential, for example, have been added since, although most of the education programmes seem to focus on the original list of seven intelligences.

The first seven intelligences proposed are:

1. Linguistic intelligence (language)

2. Logical-mathematical intelligence (mathematics and sciences)

3. Bodily kinaesthetic intelligence (physical)

4. Musical intelligence (music and rhythm)

5. Spatial intelligence (space)

6. Interpersonal intelligence (interpersonal skills, leadership skills)

7. Intrapersonal intelligence (ability to reflect on oneself)

The perspective on domain-specific ability, proposed by Gardner, appeals to many educationists for a number of reasons. First, because it acknowledges children's multiple talents and is more practical in terms of making provision. A child may demonstrate one or more of the intelligences or show outstanding performance in one area. Second, there is no ranking of the intelligences, thus encouraging us to celebrate all abilities; teachers with whom we have worked, have often felt comfortable with this model, as it provides a framework for a flexible identification system. Gardner himself recommends that creative and stimulating programmes and resources should be provided to enhance the development of these intelligences.

We believe that Gardner's theory of MI offers a sound and practical framework for assessing children's particular abilities. Teachers and headteachers we have worked with over the past 20 years have embraced Gardner's work enthusiastically.

Gardner's theory is one of the most important reference points when we make judgements about children's giftedness, talent or special abilities. Here, I am presenting our interpretations of Gardner's (1993)[2] views as articulated in our previous publication (Koshy and Casey, 1997).[28]

For exemplification of these intelligences, I have used Gardner's examples of well-known people, who have made significant contributions to their societies. It may be interesting for you to think of any children or adults you know, who may fit these different descriptions.

Linguistic Intelligence

Children who are described as linguistically gifted appreciate the order, meanings and rhythm of words. They may enjoy the challenge of decoding the rules of grammar, inventing new language and playing with words. They have extensive vocabulary and enjoy communicating. Gardner uses T.S. Eliot as an example of someone who possesses this gift. Elliot created a magazine called *Fireside* when he was just 10 years old. In a three-day period, during a winter holiday, he created 10 complete issues of the magazine.

Musical Intelligence

Those who possess this intelligence are often sensitive to rhythm, pitch and timbre and appreciate timing and tone. They enjoy both creating and listening to music. They can often recognise melodies with stunning accuracy. Yehudi Menuhin is an example of someone with this kind of talent, whose remarkable gift for music manifested itself even before he touched a violin.

Spatial Intelligence

A person who is able to perceive the visual world, and make representations of parts of it, may possess this intelligence. Pablo Picasso is given as an example of someone who possessed this intelligence. The ability to create mental images and use them in unfamiliar circumstances is also a feature of this intelligence.

Logical-Mathematical Intelligence

The use of logic, deduction and reasoning is characteristic of this intelligence. Those who exhibit this kind of intelligence are good problem-solvers. They also display powers of categorising, calculating, hypothesising, experimenting and developing arguments. Einstein is an example of someone who possessed this intelligence.

Bodily Kinaesthetic Intelligence

A person with this type of intelligence will have the ability to use his or her body to express an emotion (such as dance) or to play a game (such as a sport) or to create a new product (such as inventing) – these are all evidence of resourceful use of one's body. Martha Graham, the dancer and choreographer, is an example of someone who possesses this high degree of bodily kinaesthetic intelligence.

Interpersonal Intelligence

Gardner describes people with this intelligence possess the ability to notice distinctions between people, contrasts in their moods, temperaments, motivations and intentions. Such people are likely to be more empathetic, and more effective leaders, organisers and managers. Mahatma Gandhi, who won the respect of millions of people for his influence with non-violent protests, is an example of someone who possesses this kind of intelligence.

Intrapersonal Intelligence

Those who have good insights about their own emotions and are capable of labelling and discriminating between them, as well as drawing on them to guide their own behaviour, have intrapersonal intelligence. People with this kind of intelligence have a heightened awareness of their own strengths and weaknesses. Sigmund Freud is cited as an example of someone who had this kind of intelligence.

It is possible that while reading these descriptions you were trying to match the seven intelligences to famous personalities from the past and present. Try thinking about your child and perhaps others you know, and consider what intelligences they exhibit.

One strong message we have, for both parents and teachers, is you will only observe these different intelligences if you provide opportunities for the children to demonstrate them. How Gardner's intelligences may be used as an initial checklist for identifying children's individual strengths is discussed in Chapter 3.

Case History: Jonathan, 6 years old

During a school visit in the north of England, 6-year-old Jonathan told me that he thought he had 'bodily kinaesthetic intelligence'. He explained that his teacher told the children what they were good at, and called it their special intelligence. He explained that, if he tried really hard and practised, he might become a world-class football player. The teacher had discussed the children's particular interests individually and in groups (sometimes with their parents present). She had witnessed a rise in self-esteem, motivation and enhanced all-round achievement and effort in most children. The discussions prompted Jonathan to ask for homework and reading books to take home as he felt he needed to improve his reading and writing too.

Having said this, a word of caution here – it would be very unwise to match children exclusively to certain intelligences or to think that they may possess only one single intelligence. Many children are likely to show combinations of the intelligences in various degrees.

Carol Dweck on the Use of Labelling

The eminent Professor Carol Dweck (2006), who we have already mentioned, has concerns about giving children the label *'gifted'* as it may lead them to develop a fixed *mindset*.[29] She feels that by telling children that they have been given a *gift* makes them feel special. Dweck's worry is that some children may become so focussed on showing that they deserve the label, that they stop challenging themselves and avoid situations that may reveal their inadequacy and show that they do not have the gift.

Dweck's advice is that, if parents want to give their children a gift, the best thing they can do is to teach them to love challenges, be intrigued by mistakes, enjoy effort and keep on learning.

Our Own Ability Continuum Model

We have considered a number of conceptualisations of ability and presented a range of views and models from experts in the previous sections. Here we present our own simple *Ability Continuum Model*, which we think is a useful strategy for practical purposes.[28]

This is illustrated as a simple model in Figure 2.2. Instead of having an able and non-able, or gifted and not gifted, group – whatever method is used to measure or observe it – we believe it is better to focus on the needs of all pupils and make appropriate provision when you recognise special abilities and aptitudes displayed in different domains. This ability continuum consists of a straight line with a noteworthy feature – there are no points indicated on it to show any points of demarcation. This model takes into account the fact that ability is changeable and the best strategy is to provide the best possible learning experiences to children, which will enable them to demonstrate their special gifts and talents and potentially move towards the right of this continuum. There are no gifted and non-gifted children in our model. As mentioned earlier, there is evidence to suggest that intelligence is not fixed and can be increased given the right circumstances.[29]

Able　　　　More able　　Exceptionally able

Figure 2.2 The Ability Continuum Model.

Overview of Emotional Intelligence

One definition of emotional intelligence is from Andrew Coleman in the *Oxford Dictionary of Psychology* (2008):

> '*Emotional intelligence can be defined as the ability to monitor one's own and other people's emotions, to discriminate between different emotions and label them appropriately and to use emotional information to guide thinking and behaviour.*'[30]

Emotional intelligence is thought to have been described first in the mid-1960s. In the mid-1990s, Daniel Goleman, in his seminal work, *Working with Emotional Intelligence*, internationally popularised the concept.[31] Goleman highlighted that:

> '*We are being judged by a new yardstick which is not just by how smart we are or by our training or expertise but also by how well we handle ourselves and each other.*'[31]

In essence, Goleman and others in the field explain that success also focusses on personal qualities, such as initiative, empathy, adaptability and persuasiveness. In the context of this book, we believe that at the same time as nurturing your child's gifts and talents, whether it be in mathematics, science, sport or music, we should be simultaneously helping children to build resilience and meeting the challenges of daily life with confidence. We will discuss how to help and support aspects of children's mental wellbeing and mental health in Chapters 6 and 7.

We know a highly intelligent and intellectual person, from a poor, working class family, who through self-motivation and hard work, excelled in mathematics and obtained a PhD from Oxford University. Yet, for several years in his career he was rather unhappy and unfulfilled professionally. During conversations with people he respected and trusted, he realised that in addition to all his existing qualities he needed to actively develop his emotional intelligence, become more self-aware and aware of others. The intelligent, kind and caring person that he was had unfortunately not been recognised at work. Since he started working on his emotional intelligence, he has progressed at work, has been recognised for his other qualities, and now feels happy and fulfilled. We believe that the personal qualities that we describe as *emotional intelligence* need to be encouraged and developed from an early age and parents have a fundamental role to play.

Key Points

In this chapter, we have discussed the following key points:

- There is no universally agreed definition for the terms *'gifted'* and *'talented'*.

- There are different viewpoints and interpretations of the concepts of giftedness, talent and high ability.

- Being aware of the range of views of international experts should support your own learning about the complex ideas of giftedness and ability, as it did ours.

- Professor Howard Gardner proposes that people may possess a range of different intelligences and that this is not a single measurable concept.

- Instead of asking: *Is my child gifted?* we should ask, *What is my child's gift?*

- How 'gifted' education has developed over the years internationally and in England.

- Our own *Ability Continuum Model* provides a way of viewing high ability as not being fixed, but as a developing concept.

- The importance of *emotional intelligence* for happiness and success.

Chapter 3:

HOW DO YOU FIND YOUR CHILD'S GIFTS AND TALENTS?

Valsa Koshy

• •

The previous chapter provided an overview of the theory and background to giftedness. This chapter focusses on the practical aspects of identifying your child's gifts and talents. I provide a number of case histories – of children, adults and well-known people – to highlight and exemplify how gifts and talents show themselves and how they can be identified in practice. I also provide insights into the teacher's perspective, where relevant, to help you see *the other side* of education. I have never met a teacher who did not want the best for every child in their class and what I hope this chapter highlights is that a four-way partnership between parent, teacher, school and child is the most successful and fruitful strategy for the most positive outcomes for everyone involved.

I am convinced that rather than labelling children, we need to identify their special aptitudes, particular gifts and talents and then nourish their interests in order to maximise educational opportunities for them. In this chapter, I offer practical guidance in identifying the domains in which children display high ability, placing children at the heart of the process. I present a range of ways to identify children's special gifts and include case studies of children I have worked with. Many of these children were referred to me either by their schools or their parents.

Creating a Child's Web of Attributes

Here is an interesting practical task that I regularly undertake on courses for teachers. I ask teachers to think of a gifted, talented or able child they know, write down a few phrases or words to describe them and think about why they selected that particular child. I ask them to create a *web*, including which attributes guided them in their selection. Figures 3.1 and 3.2 show two examples of what they produced.

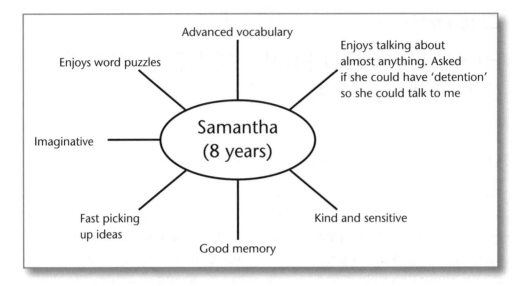

Figure 3.1 Samantha's web.

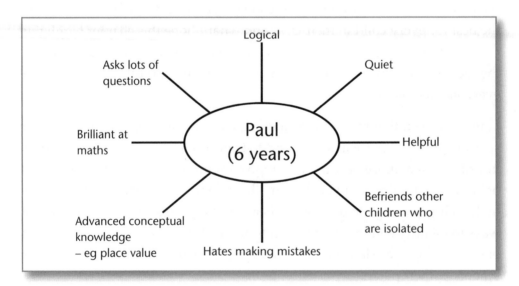

Figure 3.2 Paul's web.

Figures 3.1 and 3.2 show profiles of very able pupils in their classes, provided by two different teachers. It is possible that the characteristics listed may not be what most people would often associate with gifted, talented and very able children. Observe the type of attributes listed in these webs. Are they based on the children's performance in school subjects? Are they also based on personality traits, behaviour-related or referring to learning styles? Or a mixture? Out of 400 teachers who completed these, no child has ever been described as gifted in all areas.

Quite often, teachers do this in groups, and it makes a very interesting exercise for them to compare the lists of characteristics afterwards with those of others. We did find some similarities in teachers' lists, but not enough for us to generalise or to generate a definition of a gifted or talented child. This shows us why teachers find labelling children a very complex process.

A Potential Gender Bias?

One interesting, but serious, aspect the university team regularly found was that teachers were more likely to choose boys than girls for gifted programmes. Our colleagues in the USA tell us that there has been a similar imbalance in the number of children being selected for gifted programmes in that often a smaller number of girls compared with boys have been nominated. Why do you think this is?

In the following sections, I have included case histories of children for you to consider.

Understanding Your Child's Gifts and Talents

The most intriguing aspect of gifted education is that although there is no universally agreed definition for the word 'giftedness', there is agreement internationally that all children deserve to be educated in such a way as to enable them to realise their full potential. In a popular book on *Gifted Children*, Lucas and Claxton (2010) argue that the mission should be to *'enable everyone, without exception, to develop all their talents to the full and to realise their creative potential'.*[1] However, the concepts of developing potential, gifts and talents remain a complex challenge for many. A study by Thomas *et al.* (1996), which I presented to a policy development group at the DfEE prior to the launch of the 1999 policy, had shown that teachers in England felt uneasy about the use of the term 'gifted' to label children.[2] In 1998, Joan Freeman, an eminent British psychologist and expert in gifted education, also highlighted that the term gifted could be *troublesome* in her review of international education research on very able children.[3] Freeman's research (1991) identified the power of the image behind the word gifted and warned that such labelling needs to be used with great care, not only because it has an effect on the pupil's self-image, but also because it alters the attitudes and behaviours of others towards the pupil.[4]

Insights into a Teacher's Perspective of Spotting a Child's Gifts and Talents

In order for it to be workable, the process of spotting children's talents should be quite simple for teachers. In his book, *The Challenge of the Able Child*, David George (1992) gives examples of famous, creative and imaginative people who were not recognised by their contemporaries or their teachers.[5] He gives examples of school reports of some people who we would all agree to have made an outstanding contribution to the world. We have also followed up some of these stories ourselves.

- Albert Einstein's school report described him as *'mentally slow, unsociable and adrift forever in foolish dreams'* (George, 1992). *The Scientific Journals International* reports that he did not speak until he was 4 years old and did not read until he was 7 years old. He was expelled from school and was refused admittance to the Zurich Polytechnic School.[5,6]

- Roald Dahl: According to George (1992), Roald Dahl's school report said, *'The boy is an indolent and illiterate member of the class.'*[5]

- Winston Churchill: As a student, *'Churchill performed poorly in virtually every subject, except history and English composition.'* He was particularly inept at foreign languages. In a memoir, he described taking a two-hour-long Latin test that he left completely blank apart from his name and the number of the first question, together with a blot and several smudges.[7]

- Isaac Newton: *'did not do particularly well in school either'* (George, 1992).[5]

- Professor Stephen Hawking was not considered an outstanding student at school and did not obtain very high grades. As Hawking shares in his autobiography and was highlighted by an article in The Independent (2014), he was never above the middle of his *'very bright'* A-stream class and he was not considered *'a star'*.[8,9] During his first year at secondary school, he was third from the bottom of his class.[10] However, Hawking focussed on other interests. He loved board games and created complex new games with friends.

If you do an internet search on successful people who left school early or did not do well in school, you will see a very long list of them. Their life stories have much to contribute to how we view giftedness.

I have had many discussions on why their teachers did not notice and recognise these talents. Some children show high aptitudes in academic subjects. Others may show special talent in two or more areas, for example, mathematics and music or creative writing and sport. Johnny, a child I had come to know very well, was described as a mathematics *wizard* but he also excelled in playing rugby and is now a successful surgeon. Whether their passion is, or is not, within an academic subject, I feel it is important that all children study and acquire a strong knowledge base and develop skills in the three core curriculum areas – mathematics, English and science – even when their passion and strong interests may not lie in these subjects.

However, identifying and nurturing children's talents are immensely powerful, not just for the children in question, but for society as a whole. In a recent article in the prestigious journal, *Nature*, titled, 'How to raise a genius: lessons from a 45-year study of super-smart children', Tom Clynes (2016) reports on an American study, which shows how much the precociously gifted outweigh the rest of society in their influence.[11] He further discusses that many of the innovators who are advancing science, technology and culture are those whose unique cognitive abilities were identified and supported in their early years through enrichment programmes such as *Johns Hopkins University's Center for Talented Youth*. At the start, the Center was open to young adolescents who scored in the top 1% on university entrance exams. Pioneering mathematicians and entrepreneurs, such as Facebook's Mark Zuckerberg and Google co-founder Sergey Brin, passed through the Hopkins Center.

In Tom Clynes' article,[11] he quotes Jonathan Wai, who says:

> 'Whether we like it or not, these people really do control our society. The kids who test in the top 1% tend to become our eminent scientists and academics, our Fortune 500 CEOs and federal judges, senators and billionaires.'

Next, I cite two case histories of young students who attended our University enrichment sessions.

Case History: Jacob, the Entrepreneur

When I welcomed a group of 20 new students aged 12–13 years to our Urban Scholars Programme (USP), I asked them why they thought they were recommended to attend the programme. Most of them said that their teachers thought that they were very bright or gifted and wanted to help them achieve good results to go to university and obtain successful jobs. However, Jacob's response was different. He said:

I am here, but I don't want to be, because my friends grassed on me. I was doing so well and have already made £500 in 10 weeks by setting up a project. I did all the maths homework given to us and sold it for £5 a week to those who wanted it. They always got the answers right. I myself didn't do the homework or deliberately made mistakes so that the teacher would not find out about my secret. But I think she got suspicious and some of my classmates grassed me up and I am here, losing my earnings and some Saturday fun. Not fair.

When I asked him if his parents knew about this, he told me:

I only have a mum and I was doing this for her too. She has always said I was very clever and will end up in prison if I did this kind of thing at school.

I wondered how I could guide Jacob's entrepreneurial talent in the right direction.

Case History: Salem, a Young Boy with Dyslexia

Salem, who was also nominated for the programme, explained that he was expelled from school for carrying a knife. When I asked him why he felt he had to carry a knife, his response was,

I am so fed up with others calling me stupid. My teacher says I am dyslexic. I am not stupid, I can do sums in my head and remember things well. My idea is to set up a business – a grocery shop – and open new ones in all cities.

When I told him that carrying a knife was not the way to go about it, he said, 'you give me another way then.'

When I asked the two teachers of Jacob and Salem, neither of them had noticed how bright and able either of these two boys were, until they were asked to observe their classes closely before sending nominations for the university programme.

At the end of my lectures, I invite comments and questions from the teacher trainees about the process of spotting children's special strengths. They often say that they recognised how complex it is to spot children's special strengths, but vowed not to miss gifted children in their care. The final comment was from Nassem, a student teacher, who was also a mother of two children herself:

The problem is, what if the children don't give teachers any ideas about how clever they are or what they are clever in. I think I will keep communicating with the parents of the children in my class. I am also sure that my own kids' teachers don't know what they are clever at. So I must tell them.

 The teacher's challenge:

With classes of about 30 children and a tight curriculum to wade through, it can be incredibly hard for teachers to identify children's gifts and talents. As a parent, you could consider highlighting any specific areas to your child's teacher if you feel comfortable in doing so and think this could help.

Identifying Gifts and Talents – A Special Case for Younger Children

A few years ago, I worked with teachers of younger children, who helped me to design a set of characteristics shown by very able younger children, which they felt pointed to their special gifts. You are not likely to see all of these attributes in any individual child, but it is nevertheless a useful list.

The following attributes are often displayed:

- a high level of alertness
- making connections
- matching things
- curiosity and asking lots of questions

- very good memory
- interest in pictures and books of particular topics
- being strategic and competitive in playing games (cheating to win too!)
- interest in adult conversations
- learning, picking up ideas quickly in areas of interest
- fascination for unusual things
- highly imaginative play

Although the whole issue of identification is strewn with difficulties, we think it is important to support the notion of early identification of children's gifts, whether they demonstrate several different abilities or show an individual, specific strength. At a national conference for teachers of children aged 4–7 years, I proposed the following arguments to justify this statement.

- The first years of schooling constitute a very important stage in children's lives when interests are developed and attitudes formed. We cannot afford to make mistakes at this very crucial stage of their development.
- Mastery of facts, skills and conceptual understanding at this stage is important to support a robust framework of knowledge. Gaps at this stage can lead to serious under-achievement later in their education.
- Research has shown that high-quality early years programmes can make a significant contribution to children's attitudes to learning and in their achievement (Sylva, 1994).[12]
- Brain function research (Rutter and Rutter, 1992) suggests that we can make a significant change in children's learning potential in the first few years of their lives.[13]

Developing a Child's Interests and Passions – Case Histories

Based on a large research project funded by the government that I led with teachers and advisers in 14 local districts (Koshy *et al.*, 2006), some case histories now follow that show what can be achieved in ordinary classrooms.[14] However, the messages are equally applicable to parents who wish to help their children.

The following case histories of children were gathered during this project and from other opportunities to illustrate a range of success stories, as well as challenges faced by parents and teachers.

Case History: Melissa and Her Love of Butterflies

Melissa, a 4-year-old, who always insisted she was nearly 5, was described as dreamy, not communicating and often withdrew from all the activities in a Reception classroom – until one day, quite by chance, Melissa's teacher spotted her looking through a book that had pictures of butterflies. The teacher asked Melissa what she was looking at. Melissa excitedly told her about her interest in butterflies and her face became animated. The teacher decided to use this opportunity to make Melissa *come out of her shell* and asked her to start a project – to write about what she knows and find out about butterflies and draw pictures in a *special* book. The results were stunning. The teacher explained a *quiet dreamer* became a *passionate worker* and started communicating with both her classmates and the teacher. The parents noticed the change – they also recognised one important message – if you focus on children's interests and their passions – the results can be very significant. Ask your child about their interests and let them follow that interest – you will soon spot their gift or talent – through developing their personal interests.

Case History: David, the Stamp Collector

David, as a 5-year-old, showed a passion for collecting stamps that was always encouraged by his parents and led him to be invited to deliver a presentation in a museum. David's passion developed as he grew older and helped him to aspire high. He is now predicted to obtain high grades in his public examinations and is expecting to join a prestigious university to study Geography and Environmental Sciences. He is said to have impressed his interviewers with his knowledge of international affairs and the environment, which they felt were intellectually very advanced.

Case History: Natalie's Story – Gifted and Talented?

Natalie is 7 years old. She is bright. She is one of the first ones to finish work. She is a neat worker and conforms to all the rules in the class. Natalie's mother recently heard that in a neighbouring school they have a Gifted and Talented (G&T) programme and very bright infants are allowed to attend a special maths club after school, and she wanted to know why Natalie's school does not have a programme like that. She believes that Natalie is G&T and she deserves better provision. Natalie's teacher and teaching assistant agreed that she is bright, but not exceptional. According to her teacher, the work offered to Natalie within the classroom was felt to be adequate for her ability. This did not please her mother who is making arrangements for her to be assessed independently by a psychologist and if she 'comes out as gifted' in the test she will then 'take this up further', she said.

Think about what you would do with Natalie, if she was your daughter.

Case History: John's Special Gift of Mathematics

John attends a school in the Midlands. The following profile is constructed from his headteacher's letter. John is 6 years old and is working with a class of 7–8 year olds at the moment. He is socially immature but asks many interesting questions. He enjoys talking to the teacher and would like to share his ideas with her more often. His special strength is mathematics; in fact, he is an outstanding mathematician. He is able to solve problems quite intuitively, sometimes giving answers without writing them down. John understands the 24-hour clock and can generalise rules during investigative work. His school's headteacher says that in his 30 years of teaching he has never met a child with higher ability in mathematics than John.

But not everything is as rosy as it seems. John has very poor co-ordination. His writing skills are not well developed and, as a result, he hates writing.

He finds it difficult to accept imperfection of any sort and would rather avoid producing any work at all.

One option the school considered was to move John up to a Year 5 class.

I used this case history with teachers in a session at the university and asked them to consider a number of questions, including the ones below. There was a heated debate. Why not look at the questions and consider some of the issues that arose.

- Does John sound as if he might be gifted?
- Does moving John up to Year 5 offer a sensible solution? What might be the pros and cons?
- What do you think might help John?

John's case study highlights *asynchronous development*, whereby a child may be streets ahead academically in a particular subject, but in other ways, such as emotionally or with physical co-ordination, they are at the same stage as their peers, or perhaps even behind some of their peers.

Case Histories of Older Children and Adults

Case History: Jamil, Lost in the System

Jamil is 19 years old and works at a betting shop. He believes his secondary school failed him because they never realised that he had high ability. According to his parents, the school was situated in an urban, disadvantaged area with low expectations. There were no efforts made by the school to identify the more able pupils and target them with help and encouragement. Jamil believes he was a very capable mathematician who never had a chance to show his ability because all the lessons were targeted at the average or below average pupils. The aspirations of most of the pupils were low and he said 'no one really cared'.

Jamil feels that he was treated unfairly by a system that failed to recognise high ability, independent of social status.

I asked a group of parents to comment on this case history.

Do you think there are special difficulties associated with identifying higher ability pupils in socially deprived areas, where pupils may have low self-esteem and some schools may have low expectations of them?

Case History: Rebecca

Rebecca, aged 13 years, was described by her teacher as one of the best mathematicians the school has ever had, as her ability was exceptional. The way the school provided for her was by entering her for GCSE mathematics in Year 8. She obtained an A grade. This was felt to be a remarkable achievement by all concerned, but Rebecca started having problems after passing her GCSE. She was extremely upset that she was prevented from having any more mathematics lessons, depriving her of the most pleasurable experience in her school day. The school, which provided for 11–16 year olds, did not have the facility to offer her A-Level lessons. She also had to deal with some teachers' expectations, which Rebecca's parents described as *unrealistic*, to perform at a very high level in all subjects. Rebecca also had to endure teasing from fellow pupils for being so clever, and this made her school life unbearable. Rebecca's parents took her out of school and educated her at home. A very bouncy, alert Rebecca became moody and unhappy. Her results, aged 16 years, were three GCSE passes. She felt that if she had attended school she would have done better.

Case History: Peter

Peter was 10 years old. His parents had noticed his exceptional ability from a very young age. Among the early indicators of his ability was the way he learnt things very quickly, his use of sophisticated vocabulary and an unusual interest in Open University programmes (noticeable from the age of 5). Both his parents were Oxford graduates. Peter's teachers also identified his high ability from the start. The school felt quite confident that they could keep Peter stimulated in the classroom. This changed when Peter was 8 years old when, according to his teachers, it was clear that he was years ahead of the other children in his cognitive development. They then had to consider other strategies to teach him, appropriate to his potential.

The first solution offered by the school was to move him up three years to a Year 6 class where he would have no difficulty in coping with the academic work. His parents agreed. This was tried for a few weeks until one day Peter came home crying because he was not *chosen* to be in the class football team because he was considerably *shorter* than the rest of the class. He found no difficulty in doing the work set for Year 6 children, but felt isolated due to being physically smaller. Peter was then moved to a Year 4 class where his difference in size was not so obvious and where he felt much happier.

Moving Peter to a class where he could work and socialise with children one year older did help, but meeting all his academic needs remained a challenge for Peter's new class teacher. She felt her own knowledge of all subjects – especially in mathematics and physics – was not adequate to offer him the stimulation he needed.

Here we have an exceptionally able pupil in many subjects, whose ability was easily spotted by both his parents and school. Both made conscious efforts to nurture his ability, although educating him posed a constant challenge.

I asked teachers the following questions and you might like to consider them too.

- What feelings does Peter's situation arouse in you?
- What strategies would you choose in providing for him socially and educationally?
- What do you think Peter's needs are?

Case History: Terry, the 60 year-old Adult Acceptor

Terry drives a taxi and has taken me to various meetings and events for about a decade. Right from the start Terry struck me as a very talented adult who could be described as a *happy acceptor*. Unlike Andrew, who we described in Chapter 1, who was aware of his giftedness and high IQ and who seemed to blame others for his perceived failure, Terry was always content. However, in his primary school, Terry said he didn't learn anything – he caused no trouble and coasted along. Teachers just said he was 'lazy'.

He couldn't read and, reflecting on that period of his life, Terry thinks he must have had a specific learning difficulty, which we would now refer to as *dyslexia*, but in those days, this was not considered. Terry has always taken an interest in all mechanical things and used to take machines apart. In his secondary school, the pattern of not doing well at school continued, until a teacher took him under his wings and taught him to read. Terry's brother, in contrast, was academic, went to grammar school and obtained good A Levels and built a successful career.

When Terry left school, he worked for a large car manufacturing company and later became a taxi driver. In his spare time, he builds sheds, keeps an allotment and his own garden is immaculate. He helps friends with their gardens too. Terry frequently refers to himself as someone who 'could have been a millionaire businessman'.

Reflecting on Terry's story raised a number of points in our minds:

- The success of one teacher in encouraging Terry to tackle his reading problem, albeit later in the school years, shows the power of a teacher in tackling a problem which was hitherto dismissed.

- Terry says his parents were interested and cared about him, but they just allowed him to follow his interests in his own way. A question that arises is, would Terry's academic achievements have been different if his parents had worked with the school?

- Although Terry is a happy acceptor, is there hidden potential that he could have realised and things he could have achieved, if his talents had been nurtured?

Practical Ideas and Checklists for Identifying Children's Strengths

There are a number of things that parents can do to identify their children's strengths and to work with teachers on nurturing them. I discuss these regularly with teachers and parents and it is remarkable that these strategies work both at home and in school.

Work with the School

There is plenty of evidence to suggest that many parents notice their children's special strengths and what they can do well early in life and often before they start school. Consider talking to the teachers at school about these interests. I know of many cases where parents telling the teachers about their children's special abilities have made a difference in the quality of the children's education and levels of achievement. Parents can play an important part in identifying children with higher ability in any subject or topic. A strong partnership between parents and teachers has long been accepted as one of the factors influencing higher performance and raising the level of achievement of all children.

Take Note of School Tests

There are many kinds of tests that children take and the results are often used to assess their ability in academic subjects. One such example is the UK's National Tests, known as Standard Assessment Tests (SATs), based on what is taught in the National Curriculum. Since its introduction in 1988, there has been more awareness among teachers of children's achievements in core subjects in relation to their peer group. For example, a child who can deal with the content of the National Curriculum several levels ahead of their age, can show a capability to learn fast. Parents too need to take account of the test results and use them as one source of useful information in the assessment of ability. However, there may be changes to SATs in primary schools in response to teachers' and parents' comments.

A teacher once explained:

I will never forget the shock I had on the day 7-year-old Lilly completed her tests in a quarter of the time everyone else took. A flabbergasted me gave her the test from a higher level; she did that too in 20 minutes. When I got over the shock, I told Lilly that I was very pleased with her work and asked her why she did not do such good work every day, to which she replied: Well, my mum told me we will be doing these tests this week, you see. I thought I better try hard just for today.

It seems that Lilly was a very capable child, who chose not to show her ability at other times. The reasons for this can be speculated upon. I know of many cases where children mask their abilities for fear of being asked to repeat the same type of exercises when they have completed the assigned work, or are being teased or bullied by their peers. Standardised Tests published by the National Foundation for Educational Research (NFER) and similar organisations, are also used by some schools and authorities to identify higher ability pupils.[15] Although these tests can be useful, they do not highlight gifts or talents in non-academic subjects. Furthermore, in some cases the most able pupils are such divergent thinkers that their often *creative* responses to questions may be *wrong* according to answer sheets and may be considered *odd* answers by their teachers. If a teacher is faced with this situation, a short diagnostic interview with the child may often produce surprises.

A Place for Ability Testing

As we mentioned in earlier chapters of this book, IQ tests have been used for a long time to test potential. I know examples of children where this type of testing can be useful. I know of cases where pupils with apparent learning difficulties or disruptive behaviour have been tested and the potential predicted by the test score has been useful to the teachers and parents in identifying higher ability. Many of the tests used by independent schools to select pupils are similar to IQ tests. It is often considered that these tests can be good predictors of success in examinations, but, of course, that represents only one dimension of a child's success and happiness.

Your Child's Teacher's Observations

Your child spends many hours in school where their teachers have an opportunity to observe them closely. Naturally, as a result of these observations, the teacher may notice your child's special interests and talents. However, identifying ability also depends on the kind of work set in class. For example, if a child's mathematical work in class consists of doing pages of repetitive calculations, it is unlikely that the child will exhibit his or her powers of problem-solving or logical reasoning, which are attributes of mathematical talent. Similarly, a linguistically-talented child needs to be provided contexts in which his or her interest in vocabulary, writing or grammar patterns may be explored, for the teacher to be able to make an effective assessment. An outstanding artist is not likely to be noticed in a classroom which does not actively encourage art work. Keep a dialogue going with your child's teacher while simultaneously talking to your child about what he or she is doing at school.

Ask Your Children

In one of my projects with teachers of younger children (Koshy *et al.*, 2006), one of the most effective strategies used in the classroom was to conduct weekly discussions about children's interests.[14] Children shared their interests with the rest of the class. Some children brought artefacts of what they had done at home and others brought collections of stamps, coins and pictures of their home-based activities providing insights for their teachers. As I discussed in Chapter 1, many of the parents did not know what their children's interests and passions were. So, it is really worthwhile having conversations with your children whatever age they are.

Special Attributes to Look For

Throughout the book, we have emphasised that children who exhibit higher ability are a diverse group and that generalising their characteristics is a complex task. However, parents and teachers we have worked with have told us that they have found a list of pointers to identifying high ability or aptitudes a very useful starting point. There are different ways of characterising the attributes of talented children and the list in Table 3.1, which evolved from our experience of working with very able pupils, nominated by teachers for participation in our enrichment programmes, may be useful as a framework for observation.

Table 3.1 Higher ability pupils (in any area).

Higher ability pupils (in any area)

- Often learn new ideas and concepts quickly or they may already know most of what they are being asked to learn.

Continues on next page…

Continued from previous page...

- May show dislike of repetition of concepts and of closed tasks.

- Are inclined to choose unusual methods of working.

- Are often reluctant to record things if they see no purpose in doing so.

- May be creative in offering ideas and solving problems.

- May show an unusual sense of humour.

- May resent the imposed restrictions of the timetable, if interested in a particular task.

- Display curiosity and ask more questions.

- May be prone to being perfectionists.

- Are often capable of higher levels of thinking.

- Show more analytical thinking and reasoning.

- May have a wider vocabulary.

- May show interest in ideas and concepts which are often expected from older pupils.

- Are often sensitive.

Use the Multiple Intelligences Checklist

In many parts of the world, checklists based on Howard Gardner's MI theory (1993), are being used as a framework for teachers' observations.[16] The theory of MI is a popular option because it focusses on and celebrates *all* talents and aptitudes, not just the core curriculum subjects.

If we believe that educating the whole child is important and encouraging a multi-talented society, which respects all abilities, the multi-talented checklist that follows is a sensible basic framework for observation. I devised this with teachers, based on Gardner's work. Table 3.2 provides an observation framework that can be useful for identifying strengths, which is based on Gardner's MI theory. However, a word of caution before you look at it. You are unlikely to observe any special strengths in your child if they have no opportunities to show these abilities. For example, if children are not encouraged to read and tell or create stories, how would you know if they have a special interest or aptitude in linguistic intelligence? Try and think of people you know – politicians, artists and sports personalities – and apply this checklist and see which of these attributes fit.

Table 3.2 Adapted from Gardner's Multiple Intelligences.[16]

Name of Child
Linguistic Intelligence
Enjoys activities that involve working with words, spelling games
Enjoys discussions, both factual and imaginative
Enjoys reading and has an extensive vocabulary
Shows competence as a creative writer in different types of writing: reports, stories, letters and poems
Enjoys telling stories
Shows interest in other languages and responds to the challenge of inventing language
Spatial Intelligence
Shows aptitude for constructions, designs
Awareness of space, pattern and layout
Responds well generally to art and craft work
Visualises details and perspectives
Logico-Mathematical Intelligence
Shows enjoyment of mathematics
Enjoys logic puzzles and capable of producing reasoned argument
Good at hypothesising and generalising
Bodily Kinaesthetic Intelligence
Learns new sports with ease
Uses body competently and with agility
Good body co-ordination
Competently uses motor skills
Continues on next page…

Continued from previous page…

Musical Intelligence

Enjoys musical activities

Chooses to listen to music

Strong awareness of rhythm, patterns and melodies

Can reproduce new tunes and rhythms

Intrapersonal Intelligence

Shows initiative

Knows own strengths and weaknesses

Capable of laughing at oneself

Empathises with other people's needs

Reflective and can be easily engaged in self-evaluation

Has self-confidence

Interpersonal Intelligence

Shows management skills

Shows sensitivity to others

Co-operative in groups

Shows leadership and organisational skills

I have recommended the following *Talent Recognition Checklist* (Table 3.3) at parents' and teachers' meetings, and both groups have found it very useful. I explain that children are not likely to obtain ticks for all these attributes, but the list does indicate some useful starting points.

Table 3.3 Talent recognition checklist.

Please read each item below carefully. Tick the options you may have observed.

Talent recognition checklist
1. Learns ideas quickly
2. Displays curiosity
<div align="right">*Continues on next page…*</div>

Continues on next page…

Continued from previous page…

3. Displays a good sense of humour
4. Has a good memory
5. Good factual knowledge
6. Scores highly on standardised tests
7. Demonstrates a superior capacity for reasoning
8. Has the ability to work independently
9. Competent in symbolic activity – e.g. early reading
10. Good problem-solving abilities
11. Enjoys using or making up complex rules for stories
12. Possesses a broad attention span and can be engrossed in an activity, 'if interested'
13. Shows persistence
14. Keen powers of observation
15. Interest in topics of complexity
16. Shows imagination and originality of thought
17. Enjoys leadership qualities
18. Shows leadership qualities
19. Shows boredom with repetitive work
20. Chooses unusual methods of working
21. Has special interests such as…
22. Has a wide vocabulary

Finally, the *Interests and Passions Questionnaire* (Table 3.4) can be used with your child to elicit their personal interests and passions, which you can explore and try to encourage and nurture. For younger children, you may need to ask the questions orally. Repeat it every year, to accommodate changes in your child's interests and passions.

Table 3.4 Interests and Passions Questionnaire.

Interests and passions questionnaire
Name: Age: Date:
1. What do you like doing most when you have free time?
2. What are your favourite subjects at school, the subjects you really like and enjoy?
3. Would you like to collect things? If yes, please list the things you would like to collect.
4. If you could go on excursions or outings, which places would you choose to visit?
5. What would you like to learn more about? For example, write a book about?
6. What job do you think you might choose when you leave school?
7. What would you say that you are really good at?
8. Are there any things you would like to do better?

In this chapter, I have discussed how you can identify and explore your child's gifts and talents. I have shared with you my own philosophy that **we should no longer be searching for G&T children, but, instead, for the gifts and talents in every individual child.** This new way of identifying children's multiple talents is likely to make both the parent and the child lead happier and more fulfilled lives.

Key Points

- Identifying your child's gifts and talents is a complex but a very worthwhile process.

- It is not possible to give a general definition for a gifted child. Special interests, personality traits, behaviour patterns and learning styles need to be taken into account in the talent nurturing process.

- Research has shown a potential gender bias in the selection of high ability children for special programmes, with more boys participating than girls.

- Teachers had not always spotted special gifts in their pupils who went on to make significant contributions.

- Identifying gifts and talents in younger children is very important.

- Working with your child's school has been shown to be a very effective strategy.

- Take note of school test results, they may provide useful pointers.

- Structured observations and recording of children's special interests and aptitudes have helped many children and their parents, in the talent development process, leading to successful outcomes.

Chapter 4

CREATING STRONG FOUNDATIONS TO TURN YOUR CHILD'S GIFTS INTO SUCCESS

Valsa Koshy

● ●

Intelligence is not Fixed

One day, after a lecture on nurturing giftedness and talent to teachers who were on a professional training course at Brunel University, one teacher approached me and said:

> You know all the different strategies you said we could use with children in our school are so useful for parents too. I have two children and I have been using some of them and I think our lives have been transformed. We talk more, we discuss things, we debate and argue, do the puzzles and most of all we laugh a lot together, much of television times have now turned into talk time and doing things together.

This chapter includes many of the ideas and suggestions I have shared with teachers and with many parents, and they do work, perhaps in different ways. Many of the suggestions are adaptable and can be used with different age groups.

Our brains are malleable and change in response to how we use them. The more stimulation a person receives, the more connections they make in their brain. We talked about brain plasticity in Chapter 1. The belief that a person is born with fixed intelligence that remains the same throughout their life is no longer held. We mentioned Alfred Binet, who designed IQ tests and an authority in the field, who said:[1]

> 'A few modern philosophers… assert that an individual's intelligence is a fixed quantity, quantity which cannot be increased. We must protest and react against this brutal pessimism… With practice, training and above all, method, we manage to increase our attention, our memory, our judgement, and literally to become more intelligent than we were before.'[1]

As Carol Dweck (2006), who we mentioned in previous chapters, points out, *'it is not always the people who start out the smartest who end up the smartest. With practice and application we can change our learning potential.'*[2]

As this book is for parents regarding how they can support their children's learning, I would like to introduce you to the work of Leo Vygotsky (1978) an authority among educationists, who developed the idea of a *Zone of Proximal Development* (ZPD).[3] ZPD is defined as:

> *'...the distance between the actual developmental level as determined by independent problem solving and the level of potential development as determined through problem solving under adult guidance, or in collaboration with more capable peers.'*

The ZPD is often referred to as a kind of scaffolding or support for the learner from adults.

There are many examples of how children's learning is enhanced when they work with a more knowledgeable adult. The theory of ZPD is one of the principles we apply to our university programmes for children where the adults try to encourage children out of their comfort zone and to help them reach their real potential. Knowledge and skills that seem beyond a child's capability can be achieved with guidance and encouragement from a more knowledgeable person.

Now, let us consider some of the ways you can help your children to turn their gifts, high ability or special aptitudes into achievement.

Encourage Curiosity, Imagination and Creativity

Remember that curiosity is a basis for learning. This is true for all age groups and younger children are often very curious. You may have noticed that most checklists describe gifted children as being highly curious. Wanting to find out about things, exploring new ideas, wondering and experimenting are features of effective learning experiences. *I wonder why...?* and *what if...?* are examples of two useful phrases to encourage and extend children's learning.

Asking good questions and wondering about things encourage the learning process by making more and more connections in the brain. This needs to be in addition to asking questions to test what has been learnt – which can be tackled with or without children understanding ideas in depth. Again, the eminent psychologist Vygotsky's *Theory of Zone of Proximal Development* supports the idea about the importance of adults asking the right kind of questions in order to judge the level of a child's actual and potential development and be able to offer *scaffolding* to assist his or her development further.

The quality and the type of questions we ask children make a big difference to the quality of the learning that takes place and often children's work reflects this.

A few years ago, a group of infant and nursery teacher-researchers who worked with our Centre at Brunel University carried out an audit of the kind of questions they asked their children. It was noted that a significant number of the questions that were asked by teachers started with *What…? Which…?* and so on. These questions elicited short responses. In an attempt to improve the quality of pupil responses, the teachers changed their style of the questioning to asking questions which started with *Why…?, How…?, Where…?* and *Can you tell me more about…?* The results were very heartening. The type of answers given by the children was greatly enhanced in that there was evidence of more thinking, wondering and considering different options, which are all features of high-quality learning. The examples given here were collected from young children either as tape-recordings or written down by their teachers.

A teacher asked, 'Would you rather be a bird or butterfly?'

Child (6 years old): 'I would rather be a bird because I can fly away for a free holiday. I don't want to be a butterfly because people collect butterflies and stick pins in them. But butterflies are prettier and you can see them around in your garden and enjoy them.' (You can see the rapid chain of thinking.)

Other similar questions teachers asked 5–6 year olds:

Would you rather be…

A chair or a carpet?
A bat or a ball?
A river or a bridge?
A child or a grown-up?
A pencil or a book?
A flower or a butterfly?

Below are some more examples of what teachers of younger children have discussed with 5–6 year olds. We have included children's answers and responses for you to see what thinking is going on.

When asked, 'Would you rather be a child or grown-up?', one 6-year-old child answered:

I would rather be a child because you get lots of presents. You can hide in small places. If you are old you can't get through little gaps. You live longer if you are younger.

1. Why is the sky blue?

    This question was asked by the teacher to 5-year-old children. One response was:

    Child: I think the sky is blue because God didn't want it to be green in case the animals got confused.

2. Why are people different?

    Child: People are different because we can tell each other apart. If everybody is the same, we cannot have a best friend.

These examples show that it is never too early to encourage children to 'think' and 'reason'.

Recently, I played the odd one out game with a group of 4–5-year-old children and was quite stunned by how sophisticated some of their thinking was. I started by listing:

apple, pear, orange, pencil, strawberry

and asked children to pick the odd one out and explain why they think it is the odd one. Then I asked them to come up with their lists for the *odd one* out game. This simple activity showed that training children to think, reason and make decisions can start in the early years of children's lives. Many children happily engage in these activities and their thinking is often strikingly sophisticated. A number of selective schools use these kind of reasoning questions in their entrance tests.

J.M. Barrie's *Peter Pan* books wonderfully encourage intuition and imagination – and that a child can do whatever he or she wants through imagination. Einstein once said: *'Imagination is more important than knowledge!'*

Bloom's Taxonomy

Benjamin Bloom developed a model, first published in 1956, which has remained one of the most frequently used tools for lesson planning offering children opportunities for higher levels of reasoning and challenge leading to enhanced learning.[4] Bloom's Taxonomy has been found very useful and illuminating by many parents (as well as teachers), as it can be easily used at home with all age groups. It can be used after reading stories to the children or to be engaged in discussing current topics in the media. The model presents six levels of thinking, leading to higher levels of challenge at each level: knowledge, comprehension, application, analysis, synthesis and evaluation.

The best way to consider these levels is to think about the levels of challenge involved at each stage. Activities and questions that incorporate higher levels of thinking are shown to offer more challenging opportunities for the most able pupils and help children to learn more effectively. The higher levels of the taxonomy also encourage curiosity. Rather than give a full explanation of all the levels, I present a practical summary here. This is then followed by examples of familiar topics, which show the increasing level of challenge in each of the levels. Children benefit from this model of questioning and discussion and being engaged in activities relating to them. I have tried this framework with younger and older children, and with teachers.

Knowledge

This level is concerned with learning facts. It is the basic level that asks the learner to identify, list and cite newly-acquired knowledge. This may mean repetition for some children who may already have a very good knowledge base. If not, they too must acquire facts to be able to extend their knowledge. Facts may be remembered quite easily, even though remembering them is not always accompanied by understanding of the concepts related to them. Names of characters in a story, names of planets and animals, spellings of words, mathematical symbols and number names can be classified under this category. We know of children who can memorise and recite all kinds of facts, but do not really know much about them.

Comprehension

This level is about being able to explain the facts that have been learnt. Children can describe or summarise what has been learnt, answer questions based on a story or passage they have read or listened to.

Application

At this level, children can be asked to make use of what they have learnt and apply their knowledge in practical and problem-solving situations. This level requires a higher level of demand on their thinking and most children are often capable of taking tasks to complex levels or can be trained to do so.

The next three levels are often referred to as the *higher levels of thinking*.

Analysis

Analysis is a more complex skill, which involves looking at situations and breaking them down into component parts and perceiving relationships between them. Categorising information and seeing patterns and themes emerge are analytical processes. Analysis is very useful for understanding new ideas and making strong connections between ideas. It is a more active process than the first three levels and can result in both discoveries and generalisations.

Synthesis

Teachers often refer to this level as the most creative level. It involves looking at things in a different way, asking the question 'what if …?' or *recreate* something. This level also fosters a thinking style that is more original or unexpected and encourages taking risks and creating new ideas. At this level, children take up the challenge of designing something unusual and new and view it very positively. A question such as 'Would you rather be a bird or a butterfly?' or being asked to design a new animal, may lead to this level of thinking.

Evaluation

It is not surprising that this is classified as the highest level of thinking, as it involves many processes – personal reflection, assessment skills, making decisions and appraising the effects of something. Evaluating the effectiveness of products or type of thinking requires a high level of mental activity. Presentation of a personal project to others, reviewing one's own or other people's ideas and keeping reflective diaries of events are examples of this type of thinking being encouraged.

Example: Using Bloom's Taxonomy with Younger Children

Here is an example of how the six levels of the taxonomy can form the basis of designing questions relating to a fairy tale for younger children, *Goldilocks and the Three Bears*.

Levels	Examples of questions/activities
Knowledge	Can you make a list of the characters in the story?
	Where did the three bears live?
	What did Goldilocks eat at the bears' home?
	Make a poster showing the number of chairs and beds in the bears' house.
	What was the colour of Goldilocks' hair?
Comprehension	Can you tell the story in your own words?
	What happened to Baby Bear's chair?
	Can you draw a picture to show what happened in the story?
	Why did Goldilocks like Baby Bear's porridge and his bed the best?
	If Goldilocks had dark hair what would you call her?
Application	Find the characters in the story in a word search.
	What would have happened if Goldilocks came to your house?
	Find another bear story, read it and tell us that story
	Make up a conversation about what happened in the house when the bears returned home.
	Make a model of the three bears' house.
	Find out what you can about bears' hibernation.
Analysis	Which part of the story did you like best?
	How are bears different from other animals which people keep as pets?
	Why do we have teddy bears?
	Can you think of some reasons why everyone should have a toy bear?
	Ask 10 people in the class how many toy bears they have at home. Make up a tally of the numbers to display this.
	Find out what kind of food bears eat and think up a recipe for making a nice dish for them.

Continues on next page...

Continued from previous page...

Synthesis   Can you think of a different ending to the story?

Write a letter to Goldilocks pretending you are the Baby Bear.

Invent a new bear character and write some sentences to tell an adventure he or she might have.

Make a recording of your story and, using a glove puppet, tell the story to others.

You have been hired to design a new home for the three bears using your choice of materials. What would that new home look like?

Evaluation   What did you think of the story?

Daddy Bear was caught by bad people who used him to do tricks in the street during the day and tied him up at night. Write a letter to a newspaper to show how unfair this is and how the rest of the family feels.

Write the story of the three bears as if it happened in the present.

What kind of an animal would you like to visit you? By magic, it has learnt to talk.

Example: Using Bloom's Taxonomy with Older Children

Knowledge

This is mainly about remembering facts and giving answers. Examples:

• What political party is in power now?

Comprehension

This level of questions will involve some understanding and description. Examples:

• Can you explain how the country decides which party comes to power?

Continues on next page...

Continued from previous page...

Application

This level would involve some application of the facts you know and found out. This level also involves more thinking. Examples:

- What are the main differences between the major political parties?
- Which party would appeal to you more?

Analysis

This level involves thinking in much greater depth. You would break down the information, compare and contrast and make decisions. Examples:

- After studying the main principles of the major political parties, which one would you support? Explain why you made that choice.
- What are the advantages and disadvantages of a country having a large population?

Synthesis

This level moves away from what you know and have learnt, to new ideas and speculations. Creativity is at its highest at this level. Examples:

- If you could write a manifesto for an ideal political party, what would it contain?
- Make a presentation arguing your case.

Evaluation

At this level, you will make decisions after thinking about different sides to a story and justify your decisions. It is about making judgements. Examples:

- What do all the political parties have in common in their manifestos and why do you think they have opted for these common elements?
- If you could choose to live in another part of the world, where would it be? Why?

Helping Your Child to Develop the Ability to Think

Children who have gifts or aptitudes in any particular area show higher powers of what is usually referred to as *higher order thinking*, which involves analysing, creating and evaluating ideas. The ability to think critically, raise questions and make sensible conclusions and decisions is a mark of the intellectual capability of a child in any area and it goes without saying that we should encourage these skills to develop. This not only helps children with their school work, but also prepares them for everyday life.

I can recollect many occasions when parents and teachers have told me how they have engaged in discussions with their children of different ages. I have given some examples which should give you an idea of how you may want to start to help your children to *think* more.

Encourage Your Child to Think Critically

In a recent article in *Times Higher Education*, the former Archbishop of Canterbury, Dr Rowan Williams (2016), made a statement that resonated with our thinking and practice for over 15 years.[5] He said that universities should *'give students a good set of questions they want to be asking'* so that they can own what they are doing. This will allow students to expand their own awareness and critical skills and help them to make their own decisions. Thinking and thinking about thinking are skills we can and need to train our youngsters. This process, we believe, should start as early as possible.

Critical Thinking needs to be learnt and practised. At its essence, it is to think about topics and decide what to believe and what decisions to make. When the concept is first introduced and practised, many children shout at each other and most of them are unable to listen to each other fully. However, as time passes, students begin to listen more and propose clear, intelligent and thorough arguments.

One mother told me that our Critical Thinking lessons have helped her daughter, Natasha, 'to think more deeply about things, put forward arguments for and against things.' She went on: 'I believe Natasha is developing a sense of balance in viewing things. But, mind you, it hasn't helped in some ways.

When I tell her to do something, she comes up with arguments why she shouldn't do it'.

The majority of children who attended our programmes found Critical Thinking sessions the 'most useful' as it helped them to think more clearly, search for explanations and consider the two sides of arguments. Some students told us that their Critical Thinking skills helped them to resist joining gangs or planning and carrying out illegal activities.

In my experience of working with children, training children to think critically encourages them to develop stronger personalities, withstand teasing and bullying, seek truth and be more tolerant to the views of others.

Critical Thinking Ideas for Younger Children

Here is an example of teaching Critical Thinking skills to younger children:

You all know the story of *'Jack and the Beanstalk'*?

> *Have you ever thought that it wasn't very fair how Jack was the thief, but it was the giant that ended up dead?*
>
> *What would you do if you were Jack?*
>
> *What if Jack wasn't Jack, but Joanna instead? What if the giant was a woman and so the giant's husband was a man? How would that change the story?*
>
> *Can you think of another ending for the story? Perhaps Jack and the giant could become friends instead of enemies.*

I spent some time with younger children who were discussing these questions. These generated a significant amount of debates, agreements and disagreements. A common theme which came out was about the morality of the story in that the giant did not deserve his fate or to be punished!

Here are some more activities you can try with younger children:

1. Start a story 'Once upon a time, there were two children and two animals...' and let the child continue the story.
2. Play the 'Guess my animal' game and give progressive hints. For example:
   • My animal has a furry coat.

- People keep it as a pet.
- It likes to eat carrots.
- It has very long ears.
- Guess my animal.

3. Make up a play about a story you are familiar with. Try to change the ending.

4. Talk about favourite TV programmes and ask children why they like them.

I have used the following statements with 8-year-old children. In advance, you need to explain that it's okay to disagree and that people can think about things in different ways, but it is important to understand why someone thinks in a certain way.

- *Children should be allowed to go to bed at a time they choose.*
- *You should do everything your friend tells you to.*
- *Children should only have three toys to play with at a time.*
- *When you find something difficult at school, you should go to the teacher straightaway.*
- *If you make a mistake, it means you are not clever.*
- *If you lose a game, you should sulk.*
- *Sports keep you healthy.*

In the next chapter, we give more practical ideas for turning your child's potential into high performance.

Key Points

- Intelligence is not fixed. You can become more intelligent with more stimulation to your brain.
- Discussions help children make stronger connections in their brain and understand ideas in more depth.
- We need to remember that we can enhance children's learning power by engaging them in higher levels of thinking and questioning.
- Working with an adult or more knowledgeable person helps to bring children out of their comfort zone and challenge their thinking.

- Bloom's Taxonomy of thinking levels is a helpful framework for engaging children in higher levels of thinking.

- Critical Thinking is known to support children to develop logic, reasoning and decision-making.

Chapter 5

MORE PRACTICAL STRATEGIES TO BOOST YOUR CHILD'S POTENTIAL

Valsa Koshy

● ●

In the previous chapter, I described the action you, as a parent, can take to help your child develop thinking skills, be more creative and learn better. Here are some more ideas that I have developed based on what parents have told me are effective strategies they have tried.

Working with Schools as a Partnership

From the many conversations I have had with parents, one point that stands out is that when parents and schools work together, the educational, social and emotional outcomes for the children are more positive than otherwise. I have observed great success among children whose parents have made schools aware of their children's particular strengths and passions at different stages in their lives (as we know, children's interests and aspirations change over time). Yet, in many cases, strong interests and aptitudes displayed in the early years do seem to stay with them.

Learning Together at Home

Many parents believe that children go to school and that is where they should do all the learning. It is true that they learn at school, but children do spend a lot of time at home too and mostly with their parents, carers or grandparents. In my experience, parents often notice aspects of their children's particular interests and strengths even before they start school and throughout their school life. This is usually only the case if some other conditions are also met. Here are some of those conditions.

1. Parents should spend time with their children to discover what their interests and special strengths are. It does not mean having to spend hours

of your time, but spending *quality time* and spending it frequently is what is important.

2. Provide a rich environment at home. One grandmother told me about her 8-year-old granddaughter, Seena, who showed a strong interest in different countries of the world. Seena's parents bought her books about different countries, books on flags and capital cities. She spent hours in her room studying these and could soon memorise the capital cities and flags of 80 different countries. She made posters of different flags, currencies and special plants that grow in different countries. She entered a national competition and won a prize. Seena's parents could afford to buy the resources she needed. However, this is not the case for a significant number of parents. Please be reassured that providing this kind of support does not mean spending large amounts of money buying books and toys. Some parents have joined libraries to borrow books or use the internet. Others go to charity shops and jumble sales to buy useful books, puzzles and games.

3. Talking together about stories, puzzles and games is also essential, not only for enriching learning, but also to create opportunities to spot children's particular gifts.

Here are some practical points that can help.

Practical Ideas to Help Your Child

Read Together

Encourage children to read. This is one of the most important ways children pick up general knowledge, develop their vocabulary and writing style. This should help them succeed in school and life, in general. Reading together can start from a very young age. Start by reading to your child and let them look at the pages with you. Read the same books several times and you should see the interest building up. I remember occasions when young children (18 months to 2 years old) notice you missing a page – you can try to do that deliberately! Quite often children show their particular interests while you are reading story books or factual books. Parents have told me about children who showed strong interests in topics such as stars, aeroplanes and insects while they were very young and these interests developed over many years afterwards, in some cases leading to selecting future careers.

Talk and More Talk

I know from many years of research that *talking* about ideas with children helps them to build strong structures of understanding – even of complex topics. By talking together, I do not mean keeping a separate time for talking. Talk about everything you do together – whether it is a train journey, cooking, gardening or shopping. If children watch television programmes, you have many opportunities to follow up the ideas in real life. Recently, I heard a 3-year-old talking to her mother in the shop telling her about drinking milk 'making people's bones strong' and 'meat helping children grow healthy'. When I looked at the mother with some curiosity, she told me they had talked about healthy foods after a television programme on CBeebies and now shopping involved discussing healthy food. Making scrapbooks about topics with pictures cut out of old magazines or using commercially available stickers provide rich opportunities to talk together and help children to learn ideas and acquire the language associated with the different topics. In a recent project, I encouraged children to talk more in mathematics lessons and found that their achievement was raised as teachers introduced more mathematical talk in the classroom. The children were still taught the same as before, but during the project they engaged in more discussion and listened to each other more. Talking helped the children make new connections and improved their understanding of ideas and become better at problem solving.[1]

Using the Internet

The internet plays a big part in everyone's lives now. Spend time together searching the internet for interesting ideas, games and factual information. Recently, a grandparent told me that her grandson, Robbie (9 years old), became *hooked* on a number game website and then they started playing together. Not only did Robbie master many mathematical names, symbols and sequences in three days, he started making a book on number patterns and looking up the biographies of famous mathematicians. His mathematics learning in school improved and he was given more challenging work in the classroom and for homework.

Parents of older students could spend time with their children looking up career choices and university rankings. One parent told me:

We looked up what people can earn doing different jobs! I think I was able to bring some realism into this activity in that one day Rebecca told me: Ok mum I can dream of becoming a pop star and making lots of money, but I will also have a Plan B if the dream doesn't come true.

Preparing Your Child to Meet Challenges in Real Life

Ten years ago, one of the boys, Joseph (aged 13 years at the time), at our Saturday programme, told me:

The Critical Thinking sessions have helped me to actually step back and think when gangs ask me to join in to throw stones at people's windows or chase younger children in the street to frighten them. I hear the thinking sessions telling me, don't do it. You wouldn't like this done to your house. Then I either walk away, or sometimes I persuade the gang not to do it – although it is harder sometimes to make others see what I mean.

Parents who help their children to become 'thinkers' can see the importance of how thinking and reasoning help their children to make better choices and meet the challenges in real life. By the way, this is not to do with how educated parents are – as we probably all know of well-educated people who have made bad choices.

Parents Living in Challenging Circumstances

Emily, a mother who lives in a deprived area of London with a high level of crime of all kinds – burglary, gangs, guns and physical assaults – told us:

I tell my boys that you just have to try your best. People like us who live in these flats with no jobs don't end up in universities or get good jobs unless you do something about it.

She wanted to help them and explained to us:

I told them about us talking together – starting with 10 minutes and increasing it to 30 minutes – about successful people and what they did to get where they are. Although I don't know how to use the computer, the boys helped me to search for famous people we know and get us print-outs of what they did and where they come from.

Emily was grateful for the idea I suggested to her of helping children to talk and think. She told me that her lack of education didn't have to stop her helping her children to achieve. Emily also outlined the sad fact that children who grow up in areas like hers often go to schools where aspirations are low and where even the most dedicated teachers find it difficult to control disruptive pupils. Very bright children then often don't obtain high enough grades to go to university and children's gifts and talents are not spotted and possibly never developed.

Ngozi, who lives on an inner-city estate, explained the challenges:

My children can't go to the street, it's not safe and I can't relax until they come back. Every knock on the door I fear it's from the police coming to tell me that my children are hurt or even worse.

Ngozi's children are 7 and 11 years old. She is convinced that the 'thinking training' she does has helped them both.

It's as though these sessions help them to come out of a space where they are held tight, with no hopes and no dreams. I see their faces light up when we discuss how your dreams can come true if you try hard. Obviously, Barack Obama is a constant topic of conversation. How he became the President of America where black people were not allowed to travel with white people not so long ago!

Ngozi believed that we can motivate our children by bringing them out of their comfort zone – this represents Vygotsky's *ZPD*, which outlines how guidance from adults and peers help children to reach their potential.[2]

Metacognition – Or Helping Children to 'Think About Thinking'

In research literature, thinking about thinking is described as metacognition.

Ronia, a mother, told me about a time when she was trying to find ways of helping her daughter, Susie, to settle into a new school. Susie had moved between popular independent schools. However, according to Ronia, Susie was in the top five children in her previous class, but in the new school she came about twentieth for science in the termly examination. Susie was heartbroken, I was told. When Susie was alone with her mother, she explained her anxieties and the particular problems she had with science and creative writing. They then listed what Susie was good at and what she found difficult about the two subjects and they planned a list of actions they could take to make things better. This included setting out dedicated revision time, borrowing books from the library to help and searching the web for ideas on how to do better in tests. They realised this would take time and effort and that they would need to be realistic with their expectations. To conclude this story, Susie came seventh in the class in the tests for science and her creative writing grades moved from C to A. This scenario shows that the time Ronia and Susie spent analysing 'how to learn better' and setting achievable goals are essential in succeeding in school – and for that matter, in life too!

The concept of *Metacognition* was developed by the American psychologist, John Flavell, in 1976.[3] The term metacognition means *thinking about thinking*. For example, a learner says I am not doing well in a subject, and it may be because of what I am doing or not doing. In order to change this, I need to seriously think about what I am doing right and what I could do better. The learner also needs to set goals or targets such as doing a clearly defined task by the end of the month. This process is more likely to lead to success than feeling miserable about shortcomings and failures and eventually giving up.

What adults, parents and teachers can do is to train children to analyse what strategies they have used and what may need to change, set realistic goals and a timeline to achieve the goals. The results are often pleasing, as the learner becomes the person in control. We have seen parents who make their children aware of their strengths and possible weaknesses in learning something – a subject, a skill or solving a problem. This helps them to develop positive attitudes to learning and motivation. I recommend training children in metacognition skills from a young age, as I have seen many successful outcomes as a result of developing metacognitive skills, in terms of higher quality of work and better grades in examinations.

When Elizabeth was young, I used to ask her about her school day.

Valsa: What did you learn at school today?

Elizabeth: Nothing. (Elizabeth's answer was always the same.)

Valsa: You mean you learnt nothing?

Elizabeth: If I said what we learnt, you will then go on asking me to tell you about everything we did in school, so I just say nothing.

Interestingly, one mother told me that she used to ask her son:

Mother: How was school today?

Son: Okay. (This was his consistent answer.)

(She changed her strategy.)

Mother: Tell me about two things you felt good about at school and anything you didn't like.

This kind of thinking, the mother explained, helped her to encourage her son to think more deeply and was much more useful for developing his strengths and spotting where help was needed.

Highly Able Children, But Under-Achieving

At least half the enquiries I have received about children who are described as gifted by their parents or teachers relate to children who fail to reach their potential. This means the child could do better. Quite often the request for help comes from parents who have had their children assessed outside school using tests – commonly IQ tests – which have shown that the child is under-performing academically.

There are many causes that can contribute to under-achievement, although one thing is sure – it causes unhappiness for the child. This is particularly the case for children who are told that they are gifted and should do *better*. It causes stress and a feeling of inadequacy. Furthermore, wasting a child's talents is always also a loss for society.

I have tried to support parents in cases of 'under-achievement' when a gifted child is brought to my attention. There are many possible explanations. Next are some of the reasons we have identified for *unrealised potential* or *under-achieving* of bright students.

Boredom

I have frequently found boredom to be a main contributing factor. Teachers have a curriculum to teach and children have to be prepared for tests and examinations. This can sometimes lead to children, who have mastered the requirements of the curriculum, being given repetitive activities that can lead to boredom. A child who has strong interests and is creative fails to see the point in such repetitive work. They may *turn off* work or, in some cases, become disruptive.

One of the ways this can be addressed is to have a heart-to-heart conversation with your child. Ask about the work he or she is doing and how they find the work. If you feel that what is set in the classroom is not challenging for your child, talk to the teacher – not in a confrontational way – about your child's and your own concerns. Find out what your child enjoys doing and suggest that undertaking a personal project on the particular topic may help. Personal projects can offer a child unlimited options to explore and with very little guidance. Other curriculum areas may be extended through the project. Working with children who have similar interests also helps. Take your child to visit places – including the library – where more relevant and real information will be available. Use the internet for information. Look up people who have achieved significantly in their adult life in areas that your child is interested in. Encourage children to attend clubs inside or outside school, as research suggests that these help to extend children's interests and skills.

Does Acceleration Help?

Some schools accelerate the learning of the most able students by teaching more advanced content. For example, in terms of the National Curriculum, a Year 5 child doing work that draws on the content from more advanced areas of the curriculum, designed for older children, can be said to be subject to accelerated content. The term 'accelerated' is also used to mean that the child has been moved up by typically 1–3 years. Here, too, the process of 'acceleration' may lead to that pupil being entered for examinations at an earlier age than is normally expected.

Those who advocate acceleration argue that this method enables fast learners to master ideas at a faster rate, by using teaching material that matches their ability. It avoids a pupil becoming bored with work he or she has already mastered. Being *moved up* because of the recognition of their capacity to learn quickly can sometimes boost pupils' motivation, alleviate behaviour problems and enhance achievement.

However, I have found that the whole issue of acceleration often generates much anxiety and confusion among parents. I believe that if a school is considering acceleration as a strategy, it should be with careful consultation with parents and, with regard to the emotional maturity and social implications for every individual pupil. I know of children for whom this strategy has not worked well, as they found their interests and even the physical sizes of their new classmates being too different, which made them feel uncomfortable.

My advice would be two-fold. First, do not suggest acceleration to the school. Second, if the school approaches you with a proposal, work closely with the teachers and the school. The most positive results are achieved in the *triad* – where child, parent and teacher work together.

Give Your Child Direction and Guidance About Their Future

Some teenagers have no idea what they want to do as a career. Although aspirations and intentions change over time, it is good to have discussions about these and how to achieve them. What qualifications are required to become a teacher, a vet, a banker or a scientist? When our team of tutors carried out a survey with 120 children (15-year-olds), 10 of the 15 who wanted to study medicine were not planning to study any sciences at A-Level.

With younger children, we know that aspirations, in many cases, can be influenced by fairy tales and adventure stories. We have found that many bright children have special aptitude and passion which drive their goals and aspirations. It is never too early to start discussing the future. Also, be realistic and be aware that some children may be influenced by what they perceive to be success brought about by fame and money. I am not saying that we should spoil the young dreams, but discuss options and the skills needed for achieving their goals.

Tell Your Child that it's Okay to Make Mistakes

Wishing to be perfect and the fear of failure often make bright children 'give up' rather than realising that life is imperfect. My suggestion to both parents and teachers is that these children need to understand and be reminded that making mistakes is part of the learning process and shows that what they are attempting involves challenges. Point out examples of successful people – scientists, mathematicians and novelists – for whom making mistakes and revising their efforts is what finally led them to success. Once, a teacher asked a class of 10-year-olds to create a book marker with, 'Making mistakes is okay. If you don't make mistakes, you are not learning.' Consider trying this approach with your child.

Be Aware of the Pressure of Labels

Being labelled gifted can affect a child in many ways and can lead to under-achievement. Children may feel under pressure to 'live up to the label' – and give up altogether. Secondly, children who are labelled gifted can be become targets of bullying and teasing. Being called a 'nerd' or 'geeky' naturally creates stress in children and, as a result, some may mask their ability and not complete assigned work. In extreme cases, we have known children making deliberate mistakes in their work. Some children who are labelled as gifted may occasionally become arrogant and 'show off' much to the annoyance of their peers and teacher. Some may also feel complacent with the award of the title and coast along.

Create the Right 'Mindset' in Your Child

In previous chapters I have already mentioned Professor Carol Dweck, who has made a significant contribution to the literature relating to the development of children's potential and the malleability of the concept of giftedness.[4] She tells us that we need to recognise that talent is often very specific; it can wax and wane over time and it can be stifled by the wrong kind of praise or well-meant encouragement. Dweck shows that many of our gifted young people today need constant praise and become afraid of challenges and fall apart when things do not come easily to them. As a result, she believes they lose their ability to grow. She reminds us that the most important task facing us today is how to develop and sustain talent by fostering a love of learning, a zest for challenge and resilience in the face of setbacks.

In her research, over many years, Dweck and her doctoral students explored the concept of *intelligence* in terms of *mindsets; fixed trait* (what they call a *fixed mindset*) versus a malleable quality that can be developed (described as a *growth mindset*) and how these influence children's motivation and achievement. They found that children with a *fixed mindset* are overly concerned with how smart they are and avoid challenges and under-perform in the face of difficulty. On the other hand, those with a *growth mindset* are more concerned with learning (rather than looking smart) and this leads them to take on challenges, value effort and shine in the face of difficulty.

Dweck has shown through her research that it is possible to change the belief that intelligence is a *fixed* trait that cannot be changed through interventions and to develop a belief that intelligence is a malleable quality that can be developed. Her concern about giving children the label gifted is that it may lead them to develop a fixed mindset. It may be because by telling them that they have been given a *gift* makes them special. Dweck's worry is that some children may become so focussed on showing that they deserve the label, that they stop challenging themselves and avoid situations that may reveal their inadequacy and show that they do not have the gift.

Dweck's advice is that, if parents want to give their children a *gift*, the best thing they can do is to teach them to love challenges, be intrigued by mistakes, enjoy effort and keep on learning.

Showing affection

Help children to develop optimism and self-confidence to overcome obstacles and barriers.

Paul Tough's book, *How Children Succeed* (2013), outlines how developing character traits such as grit, self-control, determination and optimism can help youngsters to develop their potential.[5] He challenges the concept that IQ is a key factor in a person's success. Parental warmth and support play a significant role in the development of the character traits that Tough proposes.

A key message from one of Tough's research studies is that children who grow up in challenging environments need to build resilience towards adversity. Tough quotes a paper by Weaver and colleagues (Weaver, et al., 2004), who demonstrated how rats were able to overcome stress if they had what is referred to as parental 'buffers'.[6] The study was based on the initial observations by Meaney that when scientists handle rat pups, the rat pups' stress levels increased but the pups recovered when they returned to their mothers. Those mothers *licked and groomed* them. Further experiments showed that the level of licking and grooming affected the rat pups' behaviour. The pups who had higher rates of licking and grooming did better at tests and tackling mazes, were more social and less aggressive. They also exhibited more self-control. The scientists also found this phenomenon, which they described as 'attachment', in humans. This would mean that children who were more securely attached to their parent or carer displayed more positive results. However, Elizabeth has seen many parents and carers who struggle to demonstrate physical or verbal affection, sometimes because of their own experiences when they were children, where they did not receive affection themselves. So, we appreciate that it is not easy or straightforward for everyone to do this.

In my own experience, from our programmes, parents who had a warm and caring relationship with young teenagers, have been more tolerant, more committed to their children's development and better able to respond to challenges. These parents were there to nurture their children and provide a *buffer* where the children could face challenges, progress academically and develop strength of character.

Character building can and must start early in life. This provides the inner strength for children and can lead them to more successful lives. Never forget that children, like all people, respond positively to affection and warmth; their self-esteem and confidence are boosted, which often leads to higher achievement too.

Key Points

- Work with your children's school. Let the teacher know about your children's individual interests and passions.

- Engage in a range of activities at home. These may involve talking together, reading together or searching the internet together.

- Prepare your children to meet challenges in their lives by talking and engaging in Critical Thinking activities together.

- Help your children to think about their strengths and about areas they can improve.

- If you feel your children are under-achieving, talk to them and find out why this might be so. Is it boredom or some other factors affecting their learning?

- Encourage your children to accept that making mistakes is okay and that they provide opportunities to learn from.

- Be aware of the pressure children feel with the label of being 'gifted' leading to the development of a fixed mindset and children could either become complacent or develop a fear of failure and letting their parents down.

- Help your children to develop optimism and self-confidence to overcome obstacles and barriers.

- The *attachment* children form with their parents, grandparents or carers can provide them with strength of character.

Part II: Health and Wellbeing

Chapter 6

THE ROLE OF MENTAL WELLBEING IN FULFILLING CHILDREN'S POTENTIAL

Elizabeth Koshy

● ●

Children's *wellbeing* can affect their capacity to learn, their motivation and performance. In recent years there have been a significant number of reports and policy documents about children's *wellbeing* and how it might affect their learning. Like the complexity of defining *giftedness*, there are several possible definitions for *wellbeing* and they cover considerable breadth. The term *wellbeing* is used ubiquitously, with varying meanings, and there is no universally accepted definition. Furthermore, there are numerous different wellbeing domains (e.g *social, emotional, psychological, mental, economic, life satisfaction* and *physical wellbeing*).

> **In simple terms (positive)** *wellbeing* **can be described as viewing life positively and feeling good.**

The more you read about *wellbeing* the more complex it can appear, so here I strive to present it in a more accessible way. I present my interpretation of *wellbeing* and its key domains and the relationship between them. For reference, the rather technical definitions of terms such as *health*, key *wellbeing domains* and *mental health* are included in Appendix 1. In this book, the term *wellbeing* refers to *overall wellbeing* and encompasses the different *wellbeing domains*. It represents a spectrum that includes both good (positive) and poor (negative) *wellbeing*.

Mental wellbeing is a wide-ranging theme and, within this book, I can only focus on some of the key areas, which are particularly relevant to children's happiness and development. This chapter provides some background on mental wellbeing and summarises key issues discussed in the media.

It discusses the foundations needed towards cultivating positive mental wellbeing in your children to optimise their learning power. I outline aspects surrounding *mental wellbeing* and *mental health*, and discuss the fundamental importance of sleep. Chapter 7, then talks about anxiety and stress, bullying and emotional resilience and finishes with some pointers on how you can help to cultivate a happier child. These topics are hugely relevant for a child's future contentment and success. I try to address how to navigate a child towards a state of happiness, which, in turn, contributes towards self-fulfilment. This can be challenging, but every parent's dream is to equip their children to be as happy and successful as possible.

Part II refers to some important policy documents and reports. I have included them so that when you need to find out more about a specific idea you know where to look.

Contextualising Mental Wellbeing and Mental Health

Wellbeing is a broad topic and many professionals struggle to agree on definitions and what they mean. Below I present my interpretation of some of the definitions and how they relate to each other. However, if this seems a bit overwhelming, do skim over it or go straight to the 'Facts and Figures' section.

Let me start by discussing *wellbeing* in the context of health, and the different *wellbeing domains*.

Health encompasses both *physical* and *mental* health (Figure 6.1a). Physical and mental health can influence each other, as indicated by the two-way arrow in the diagram.

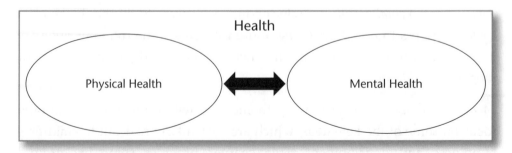

Figure 6.1a Health encompasses both physical and mental health.

Mental wellbeing

Mental wellbeing encompasses both *emotional* and *psychological wellbeing* and concerns how an individual child feels (Figure 6.1b and Appendix 1). A child has good *mental wellbeing* if he or she is happy and confident (good *emotional wellbeing*) and can manage his or her emotions in an age appropriate way (good *psychological wellbeing*). *Social wellbeing* concerns a child's interactions. A child has good social wellbeing if he or she has good and balanced relationships with other children and with adults. *Physical wellbeing* concerns whether a child feels healthy and energetic. The two-way arrows in Figure 6.1b highlight that the different wellbeing domains can influence each other. For more definitions and information please see Appendix 1.

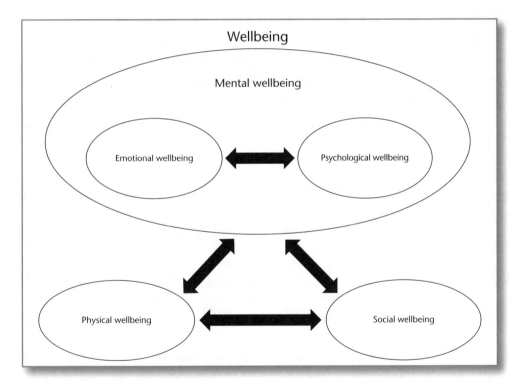

Figure 6.1b The relationship between the different wellbeing domains.

Everyone's *mental wellbeing* is *fluid* and varies over time; it can change quickly (from hour-to-hour and day-to-day) in response to positive or negative experiences. Furthermore, it is not simply a binary (two-way) state of good or poor wellbeing, there are intermediate presentations too. However, it is important to be aware of what good *mental wellbeing* looks and feels like, and to constantly work towards it. However, if children (or adults) experience low *mental wellbeing* over a long period of time they are more likely to develop a *mental health problem* or *mental illness*. So, if possible, prevention should be the goal.

Mental illness

In this book, *mental health* represents a spectrum, with *mental wellbeing* at one end and mental illness at the opposite end (Figure 6.2). This is also the paradigm (model) adopted in an academic review of the effectiveness of interventions to promote *mental wellbeing* in children in primary education.[1]

There are numerous mental health problems and illnesses of varying severity. At the more severe end of the spectrum are less common diagnoses which include: severe anxiety, depression, specific eating disorders and psychotic manifestations and diagnoses (including schizophrenia and bipolar disorder). However, different mental health problems can overlap in terms of their severity. Additionally, how they affect an individual varies considerably, as children (and adults) have different *thresholds* for being able to cope with any given problem.

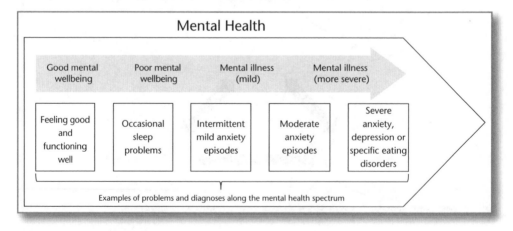

Figure 6.2: A representation of the mental health spectrum.

Some Facts and Figures

- The World Health Organization (WHO) reports that around 20% (1 in 5) of the world's children and adolescents have mental disorders or problems and about half of mental disorders begin before the age of 14 years.[2]

- The UK-based Millennium Cohort Study found over 20% (1 in 5) children experienced a mental health problem at some time between the ages of 3 and 11 years.[3]

- The Children's Society report stated that 1 in 11 children in the UK (over 500,000 children), aged 8–15 years, have low subjective wellbeing at any one point in time.[4]

- The Office for National Statistics includes 31 measures of children's wellbeing, within seven domains and found that about 12% (1 in 8) children reported being *'bullied at school physically or in other ways, or both, at least four times in the last six months'* (ONS, 2016).[5]

- The Good Childhood Report (2016) highlighted that boys are more likely than girls to experience a mental health problem at age 10 when all types are considered together – but the situation is reversed by age 14.[6]

- Girls are more likely than boys to experience emotional problems, such as anxiety and depression, as they grow older. Emotional problems are linked with perceptions of appearance and life as a whole among girls.[6]

- By contrast, younger boys are more likely than girls to be unhappy with their school work and more likely to have conduct and inattention or hyperactivity problems.[6]

These facts and figures put the tremendous need for helping children's wellbeing into context.

Effect of Mental Wellbeing on Learning and Happiness

Recently, a mother told me that she was fed up with hearing people 'going on about' the words 'mental wellbeing', that there was 'nothing mentally wrong' with her child, and that people are making 'a big song and dance' about this. Talking about someone's mental wellbeing does not suggest that there is anything wrong with them. As I previously mentioned, mental wellbeing is a positive concept about the state of one's mind and helping every child (and adult) to achieve it. It is much more about being conscious about what contributes to and distracts from a positive state of mind and happiness.

I asked 90 parents, from different backgrounds, what they wanted most for their children. Without exception, they all wanted their children to be happy, healthy, do well in school and obtain a good job. These outcomes are generally associated with positive wellbeing by most people. So, this chapter focusses on how you can help your child to achieve positive wellbeing, which is necessary for them to achieve overall fulfilment and success. Academic achievement alone is not enough for a successful life. John Cridland CBE, the former Director-General of the Confederation of British Industry (CBI), highlights in his endorsement of this book that *'gifted'* children often have poor wellbeing. In fact, even if your child is doing very well educationally, you need to ensure that they are supported emotionally to maintain their level of achievement. Your children's mental wellbeing crucially affects their learning capacity and contributes to their ability to benefit from teaching and to achieve their full potential.

The potential relationship between positive wellbeing and aspects of learning is depicted in Figure 6.3. Happy children find it easier to concentrate and learn and positive learning experiences also improve a child's self-esteem. The relationship between positive wellbeing and successful learning works in both directions. However, the converse also applies – there is similarly a link between negative or poor wellbeing and reduced concentration and other aspects surrounding poor learning. The key message is that **a happy child is more likely to be a motivated learner and an unhappy child is more likely to be a reluctant learner**.

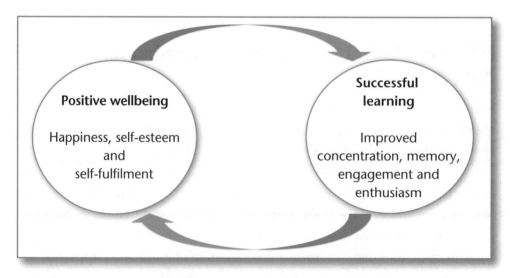

Figure 6.3 A two-way relationship between positive wellbeing and successful learning.

Some fast learners who achieve high grades in tests are still unhappy. Many lack confidence, feel anxious and may even give up on themselves and their ambitions. Sometimes, high pressure from parents, from themselves or from the school to do well academically, can create stress, which can lead to loss of interest and disengagement.

These views are based on current evidence from authoritative sources. The Department for Education's report 'The Impact of Pupil Behaviour and Wellbeing on Educational Outcomes' (2012) shows that children with higher levels of emotional, behavioural and social wellbeing tend to have higher levels of academic achievement and engagement – both at the time and later in school life.[7] Similarly, Public Health England's (PHE) report, 'The link between pupil health and wellbeing and attainment' (2014), highlights that healthier and happier children are likely to perform better academically and that school-based promotion of social and emotional skills among children is beneficial for their wellbeing.[8] The report cites a UK study which found that children's wellbeing predicted their later academic engagement and progression in school. For example, children with better emotional wellbeing at the age of 7 years obtained higher scores when they were older in their Key Stage 2 tests (aged 10 or 11-years old) than those with poorer emotional wellbeing.

In September 2014, 'The Children and Young People's Mental Health and Wellbeing Taskforce' was established to consider and recommend how mental health services are organised, commissioned and provided and how best to improve them. The Taskforce recommended *promoting resilience, prevention and early intervention, and improving access to effective support'*. It called for *'a system without tiers, care for the most vulnerable, transparency and accountability'* (NHS England, 2015).[9] Mental wellbeing and mental health service provision for children are frequently discussed in the media and are very much on the political agenda (BBC News, 2017).[10] I find it very encouraging that the national scene for mental wellbeing and mental health among children (and adults) is changing and positive steps are being made in this area.

The importance of mental health has increasingly been recognised, not just by health professionals, but also by educationists, politicians and the media. Some very useful information for parents is outlined in a report, 'Too Much

Too Soon? The Emotional and Mental Health Issues of the UK's High Learning Potential Children' (2015), published by Potential Plus UK, which supports children with high ability and potential. The report tells us that the *number of children with emotional and mental health issues is increasing*'. Potential Plus UK suggests that many of these cases are among children with high learning potential, particularly those who find it difficult to cope with:[11]

- *'increased stress levels exacerbated by their perfectionist traits;*
- *isolation and loneliness caused by lack of friends and understanding within the classroom and beyond;*
- *rigid structures within some school environments, which do not address their needs.'*

The conclusion of the report is that children, in general, are becoming more stressed in the UK. Parents are becoming increasingly stressed too! A contributing factor to this may be, in part, the increased pressure from within the school system in terms of curriculum coverage and assessments. Some reasons may include a growing emphasis on attainment and progress, sometimes at the expense of a holistic approach towards learning, which also considers the social and emotional needs of children. While many children across the spectrum face mental health issues because of this increased pressure, a child with high learning potential can be more vulnerable. Based on Valsa's and my work with parents, we believe that many children with high ability and potential can find it difficult to develop friendships, especially with their classmates. This may be because they might be seen to display some unusual attributes or are not on similar wavelengths. They can become victims of bullying and be isolated.

We even know of parents who have encouraged their child not to put their hand up so much in the classroom, as they felt that their child was being targeted for being clever and that it might appear as if they were 'showing off'.

Prince William's Perspective

Robert Jobson reported, in the *Evening Standard* (2016), that Prince William, the Duke of Cambridge, when speaking about his own family, called for adults to encourage children to talk and seek support if they are feeling down.[12] He emphasised that he and his wife, the Duchess of Cambridge, wished for their children not only to achieve their academic potential but also to feel emotionally supported too. Prince William commented that, *'For many young people, changing schools or starting a new academic year, is really difficult to deal with.'* He went on to say that, like all parents, he and his wife want to ensure that their children are also happy and emotionally supported. He proposed that parents and carers speak with children about things that worry them. The *10 Tips for Talking* (2016) on the 'Headstogether' charity website helps to guide parents to have such conversations.[13] An article on this website highlights that currently fewer than half of parents talk to children about matters potentially relating to their mental health, even though a fifth of children will experience a mental health problem by the time they are 11 years old. I encourage you to read this extremely helpful article.

Maslow's Hierarchy of Needs Towards Self-Fulfilment

Abraham Maslow, an eminent US psychologist, published a landmark paper, in 1943, called 'A Theory of Human Motivation'.[14] His paper outlined that people (including children) possess five sets of *needs*. He says, as each level of need is satisfied, then the next level of need dominates. The *first* and most basic need we have, is for *bodily functioning*, which is fulfilled through *eating and drinking*. The *second* state is the desire to *feel safe and secure*; *third* is the need for *love, friendship and company*; the *fourth* is the *requirement for social recognition and respect* and the *fifth* and final stage is *self-actualisation*. Self-actualisation is about actually fulfilling what an individual is capable of achieving. So, as a parent, your role is to strive, if possible, towards helping your child move through each of these five levels, so they can realise their full potential. This is often represented as a pyramid. I have shown it as a series of rungs (or steps) up a ladder in Figure 6.4.

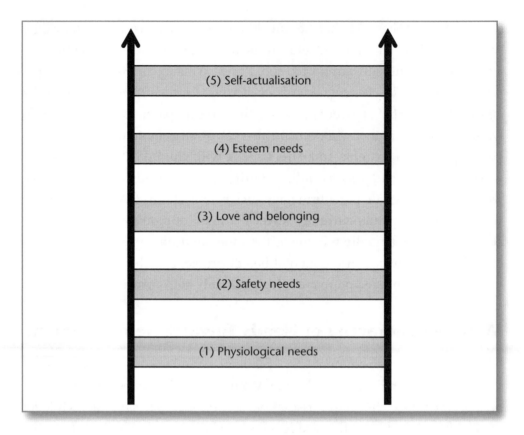

Figure 6.4: Maslow's 'Hierarchy of Needs' (1943).[14]

More Hugs!

In keeping with Maslow's Hierarchy of Needs, physical affection, such as hugs, can have beneficial effects on our child's (and our) wellbeing. When we hug our loved ones, it releases a chemical hormone called *oxytocin*, which makes us feel good and promotes *attachment* (remember those rats and their pups in Chapter 5). Oxytocin can also lower stress hormones circulating in our bodies, reduce our blood pressure, improve our mood and even increase our pain tolerance. It is a very powerful hormone to encourage in our children's and our bodies – so, if you can, try hugging more! However, as alluded to in the 'Showing Affection' section at the end of Chapter 5, background circumstances can sometimes make this difficult for some parents to do.

The Children's Society's Six Priorities for Wellbeing

The Children's Society offer a more contemporary and practical way of thinking about the elements required for wellbeing among children to enable them to fulfil their potential.

The Children's Society asked 30,000 8–16-year-olds some wellbeing questions. It is grim reading that 1 in 11 children in the UK (over 500,000 children) aged 8–15 years have low subjective wellbeing (self-esteem) at any one point in time. The organisation has researched wellbeing in children and identified six priorities for positive wellbeing. The Children's Society report, 'Promoting Positive Wellbeing for Children' discusses each of the priorities in detail.[15] The report is an interesting read if you want to find out more about this area.

The Children's Society's six priorities for wellbeing are to have:[15]

1) *'Enough of what matters.*

2) *The right conditions to learn and develop.*

3) *A positive view of themselves and an identity that is respected.*

4) *Positive relationships with family and friends.*

5) *A safe and suitable home environment and local area.*

6) *The opportunity to take part in positive activities to thrive.'*

We understand that life is not easy or straightforward and that these six priorities may be extremely difficult to achieve in many households. Therefore, your goal, as a parent, could be to work towards achieving as many of these priorities as possible.

Perfectionism

Some children who excel academically can struggle with perfectionism. Perfectionism can be a serious problem, particularly among very able children, who set very high, and sometimes unachievable, standards for themselves. Some children feel they should be excelling in every subject area and if they are not, they feel a failure. Parents (and teachers) can help by reassuring a child who struggles with this personality trait that it is fine to make mistakes and that we all learn and grow by making errors.

Case History: Charlotte

Charlotte, a 6-year-old, used to suffer greatly with *perfectionism*. She could not bear to make a mistake in anything and her *eraser* became her best friend, as it enabled her to undo her written errors. She also used to become very upset, for example, if she left an item behind, or forgot to take something into school. Seeing how much pressure she was putting on herself, her parents started to forget things and make errors intentionally themselves, so that she could see that they make mistakes too and that it did not matter. This helped enormously. She still struggles with perfectionism, but to a lesser extent.

Perceptions of Others Do Matter

Children often adulate exceptional talent in sports or entertainment, but academic talent may sometimes be resented. Playground bullying and name calling such as 'swot', 'teacher's pet' or 'nerd' can make a child unhappy and force them to mask their ability, sometimes even intentionally to make mistakes to be part of the crowd and not stand out or be deemed different. Being selected as a member of a gifted and talented (G&T) group may aggravate this situation.

Some very bright children with great creative and problem-solving skills can be unnoticed and neglected by their peers and teachers. We know of many examples of children, with high ability, who have a learning difficulty or physical impairment, and feel frustrated that they are overlooked and not encouraged. As a parent, you need to talk to your children about how they feel about learning and how they view school, to find out if there are any issues you need to discuss with them or inform the school.

Possible Consequences of Poor Mental Wellbeing

There are many reasons for children to experience poor mental wellbeing. Taking tests, and how children, parents and schools deal with external assessments, can also generate enormous pressure on children of all ages, as well as on their parents. As a GP, I frequently saw children who had 'tummy aches' or 'headaches' and, when further probed, it was clear that they were stressed about forthcoming tests. Numerous children have problems with friendships, or feel lonely or excluded. Many children I saw in hospital and general practice, pointed at different parts of their body when the actual problem they originally presented with was somewhere else, or had 'distractable pain' (by which I mean the pain they presented with was not present when they were sufficiently distracted), which suggested that the physical problem might have been a manifestation of a non-physical or emotional issue.

There is concern that the number of children and young people in the UK with mental health and emotional problems is growing. Potential Plus UK highlights in its report, that an increasing number of children with high learning potential, are experiencing more severe mental health issues, including self-harm, suicide attempts, eating disorders and depression, which require professional support. At school, mental health issues can contribute to under-achievement and lead to self-exclusion from school or certain activities.[11]

However, on the more optimistic side, you can play a major role in ensuring your child stays mentally healthy, be aware of potential challenges, handle them early and sensitively, and support them. This book will hopefully help you in that process.

Mental Health Problems Show No Discrimination

As I mentioned earlier, some parents may become alarmed when they hear the words *mental wellbeing* and *mental health*. It is easy to interpret these terms in a negative way. However, let me reassure you, supporting good mental wellbeing involves helping children to cope with the stresses, challenges and tribulations of everyday life. Although public perception is changing, the topic of mental health has been stigmatised, and often neglected, over many centuries. There is no shame in having any issue or problem on the mental health spectrum. Society is increasingly aware and attitudes are becoming more positive. Many celebrities have openly shared details of mental health problems they have had to come to terms with, ranging from anxiety to depression, and other conditions. This has positively influenced society's views and reduced stigma. Examples include Stephen Fry,[16] Catherine Zeta

Jones,[17] Will Young,[18] Robbie Williams[19] and Alastair Campbell[20]. Prince William and Prince Harry have also openly discussed the mental health challenges they both faced, following the death of their mother. The range of people affected shows that a mental health problem can affect anyone. It is very intriguing that so many actors and performers suffer from *stage-fright*, which is a form of anxiety. Unfortunately, no one is *immune* to the spectrum of mental health issues. However, help is out there to overcome or cope with challenges.

Interestingly, mental health challenges can sometimes be linked to greater determination. For example, Dame Kelly Holmes has publicly spoken about how the depression she suffered in 2003 helped to make her a more determined and focussed athlete, one year before she won two gold medals at the Olympic Games in Athens (BBC News, 2008).[21] Alastair Campbell is also quoted as saying that his depression had subsequent positive effects (BBC News, 2008).[21]

In short:

> ⭐ *Issues surrounding mental health and happiness can affect children from all backgrounds.*

Once we have acknowledged that anyone can be affected by mental health issues, our priority, as parents, is to help children develop a range of strategies on how to respond positively to adverse events and experiences, and to create an environment where they are comfortable to talk about their concerns. I will discuss this further in Chapter 7.

Sleep Matters

First, and this may surprise you, I will discuss sleep and its importance to wellbeing. Why is sleep important? The requirement for sleep is often underestimated; yet, sleep is a basic requirement for children (and adults) and good sleep contributes to positive physical and mental wellbeing, as well as aspects of learning and memory, whereas lack of sleep, or sleep deprivation, has the opposite effect.

Did you know that we typically spend about a third of our lives asleep?

Why do Children Need Sleep?

Sleep allows the body to repair itself and facilitates the brain in consolidating memories and processing information. Persistent sleep deprivation or poor quality sleep may contribute to a weakened immune system and other problems, such as anxiety and low mood. Research has shown that night-time sleep is as important for children's wellbeing and development, as healthy eating and exercise. Children who do not sleep enough may crave and eat sugary or starchy foods during the day to provide them with the extra energy required to stay awake.[22] These children are then, in turn, also more likely to become overweight or obese. To make matters worse, obesity can lead to interruptions or *pauses in breathing* during sleep ('sleep-disordered breathing' or 'obstructive sleep apnoea syndrome'), which further disrupts sleep.[23] So, it creates a vicious cycle.

How Much Sleep does a Child Need?

It is difficult to know if your child is having enough sleep, but a crude indicator is if your child wakes up and is happy and alert and ready to start the day, they probably have had enough sleep. However, if they do not wake easily or are dopey or irritable, they may not have had sufficient sleep. Of course, there could also be other issues, which need to be explored, or they might just be in a bad mood that day (like we all experience!).

This book is focussed on younger children, so I focus on the recommended sleep duration for this age group. However, if you have older children or are interested in other age groups you can explore the websites quoted in the References section (at the back of the book).

While the Royal College of Psychiatrists highlights that every child is different, it also provides a general *rule of thumb* that primary school-aged children need 10–11 hours' sleep (while teenagers need 9–10 hours, and preschool children aged 3–5 years require 11–12 hours' sleep).[24] The National Sleep Foundation recommends that children aged 6–13 years need 9–11 hours' sleep.[25] Table 6.1 summarises the guidance. As you can see, recommended sleep durations are not fully consistent!

Table 6.1 Recommended hours of sleep according to age.

Age Group	Recommended hours of sleep	
	Royal College of Psychiatrist[24]	*National Sleep Foundation*[25]
3–5 year olds	11–12 hours	10–13 hours
School-aged children	10–11 hours	9–11 hours

Sleep Problems

Although there are some uncommon medical problems which can account for sleep disturbances, mostly non-medical causes are responsible. Most children have occasional problems with sleep, and this is normal. However, if it becomes a regular occurrence, it is important you uncover any underlying physical or emotional issues, particularly as sleepiness at school affects concentration, learning, memory and overall wellbeing.

Notably, younger children who are (consistently) sleep-deprived may seem irritable and overactive and may need constant attention; they may also struggle to concentrate well.

How to Tackle Sleep Problems

Worryingly, in England, hospital attendances for 'sleep disorders' among children aged under 14 years have tripled over the last 10 years, according to NHS data analysed by BBC *Panorama*.[26] The programme proposed some possible explanations. Aside from the problems caused by 'blue light', which I describe below, the programme suggested that fizzy drinks that are high in sugar and caffeine make it more difficult for children to 'switch off' and go to sleep. It also suggested that evenings are often busier and bedtimes later in many households.

There are some basic steps you can take to tackle sleep problems. A regular and consistent bedtime routine helps many children (and parents) relax and wind down after a hectic day. Other useful strategies include not having any *screen time*, whether that is television, laptops, tablets or smartphones, at least 1 hour before bedtime. At night, artificial light disrupts our body's natural 'biological clock', which can affect sleep. However, some colours within the light spectrum do more harm than others. Blue wavelengths ('blue light') appear to be the most disruptive at nighttime. Blue light, which is emitted most intensely by smartphones and tablets, reduces the production of melatonin most significantly. Melatonin is the natural hormone produced by the body that makes us feel sleepy.

Your child's bedroom should be comfortable, dark and quiet. A bedtime story is an ideal way to complete the routine, if that is possible. This is not only calming for children, but it also fosters your child's interest in books and their desire to read for themselves. Please do read the NHS Choices website for practical tips for sleep problems.[27]

A daily bedtime routine helps to program a child's brain to enter the sleep cycle more readily. Researchers from University College London published a study, in 2013, which found children with irregular bedtimes are more likely to have behavioural difficulties.[28] They discovered that irregular bedtimes can disrupt the body's natural rhythms and cause sleep deprivation, which can affect children's ability to regulate certain behaviours. Professor Yvonne Kelly, the lead author, is quoted as saying, *'Not having fixed bedtimes, accompanied by a constant sense of flux, induces a state of body and mind akin to jet lag and this is important for healthy development and daily functioning.'* She continues, *'We know that early child development has profound influences on health and wellbeing across the life course. It follows that disruptions to sleep, especially if they occur at key times in development, could have important lifelong impacts on health.'*[28] So, it is important to think about setting a regular time for your child to go to sleep and try to stick to it, where possible.

Some children struggle with the change from Greenwich Mean Time (GMT) to British Summer Time (BST) and the switch back. One way to help is to try to gradually stagger your child's bedtime during the week preceding the clocks changing so that it is not such an abrupt shock from one day to the next. Perhaps make a diary entry for the week before the clocks change as a reminder to start this process!

Sleep checklist

Good 'sleep hygiene' is important to encourage good sleeping patterns. Here is a quick, simple checklist to follow, if sleep is a problem for your child:

✓ Is the bedroom temperature – too hot/cold?

✓ Is the bedroom – too light/dark?

✓ Is the bedroom – too noisy (e.g. from sound in neighbouring rooms)?

✓ Is your child visiting the toilet in the night? If yes, consider restricting fluid closer to bedtime.

✓ Caffeine (including chocolates and hot chocolate drinks) and sugary drinks and food are best avoided as they may make children hyperactive or over-stimulated and can make it difficult to fall asleep.

✓ Lack of tiredness due to inadequate physcial activity – please do read the chapter on physical activity and apply it!

✓ Hyper-stimulation – avoid the TV, computer/laptop, tablets and smartphones at least 1 hour before bedtime.

✓ Is your child persistently worried about anything? The next chapter is designed to help you identify and address challenges. In some cases you may need to seek expert advice.

*   *   *

There are many things parents can do to help their children cope with pressure, feel happier and be more successful. The skills and habits that parents develop with their children can contribute to their successful interaction with their immediate surroundings and the wider world around them – both now and for years to come. I hope your increased awareness of the concept of mental wellbeing will, in turn, help towards your children leading more contented and successful lives. Please read Chapter 7 to find out more about these themes.

Key Points

- Issues surrounding mental health and happiness can affect children of all ages and from all backgrounds.

- Children with better emotional wellbeing at the age of 7 years obtain higher scores in the Key Stage 2 tests than those with poorer emotional wellbeing.

- The Children's Society's six priorities for wellbeing include: having enough of what matters; the right conditions to learn and develop; a positive view of themselves; positive relationships; a safe and suitable home environment and local area; and opportunities to take part in positive activities to thrive.

- Sleep is essential for positive physical and mental wellbeing.

- Poor sleep may make children crave sugary or starchy foods.

- Persistent poor sleep may also weaken a child's immune system and make them more susceptible to common infections.

Chapter 7

PROMOTING POSITIVE MENTAL WELLBEING AND HANDLING CHALLENGES

Elizabeth Koshy

● ●

Mental health problems are diverse and entire books are dedicated to covering the wide breadth of conditions. In this section of the book, I am focussing on some of the more common issues and challenges that affect primary school children. Mental health among children and adults is now very much on the political and societal agenda. Being aware of these issues could help you notice early symptoms and address them promptly.

In this chapter, I discuss some common areas which can cause problems for children, including stress and anxiety, bullying and lack of emotional resilience, and I conclude by discussing how to help your child become happier.

Stress and Anxiety

Children experience a range of feelings surrounding what is happening to them and it is natural for them to feel worried or fearful from time to time. Anxiety can be a protective mechanism and a cue for adaptation, coping and survival. A degree of anxiety can help children to have the determination and impetus to do their best at something, but if they are too anxious it can impair their functioning altogether.

Anxiety is a common mental health problem in children. There are different types of anxiety, including: generalised anxiety, social anxiety, a specific phobia and panic attacks. Anxiety falls within a wide spectrum and can vary considerably between individual children. A small group of children experience intense and frequent – moderate to severe anxiety – episodes which can affect their daily lives and quality of life. This can affect their wellbeing and can affect their confidence and self-esteem. Children can become withdrawn or avoid certain things or situations that trigger their anxieties. All of this can affect their school and home life.

How Might Anxiety Present?

Anxiety can lead to emotional and/or physical symptoms. Examples of symptoms and signs that children might experience include any of the following.

- Children may feel panicky or fearful, experience strange sensations or pain in the chest or tummy, headaches, feel sick or tense, be fidgety or frequently need the toilet.
- They may also become unusually quiet, clingy, reluctant to go to school or somewhere else, be irritable, angry, argumentative, tearful, have appetite changes or have difficulty sleeping.
- You may notice or hear about behavioural changes at school, observe this at home or their school performance might change.
- They may lose interest in activities they previously enjoyed.

It can be difficult for a child to recognise that they are anxious and to tell you, so you need to be aware of the symptoms yourself and look out for any *changes*. The Royal College of Psychiatrists has produced an extremely helpful and concise information leaflet on anxiety.[1] NHS Choices also present some very helpful information and resources on 'Anxiety in Children'.[2] The website information for these organisations can be found in the References section.

Potential Causes of Anxiety

Several factors can contribute to a child feeling anxious – these include their genes, observed behaviour and social factors, such as experiences at school or home. Our genes may strongly influence the development of anxiety. However, we can still work on the environmental factors, which we can influence!

Home factors are numerous and include parents or carers frequently arguing. It can also be learnt behaviour if children see you or someone else in their lives who is upset or anxious. A significant life event, such as a bereavement in the family, a divorce or parents separating, parental illness or an accident can also potentially generate considerable anxiety. A frightening or a traumatic event, such as an accident, can cause post-traumatic stress disorder (PTSD) in some children, which may need specialised help.

Children with any type of *special educational need* (SEN) or *disability* are particularly recognised to be at potential risk of experiencing social problems and anxiety. If your child has a SEN or disability and is experiencing problems, you may need to seek advice from your school or other professionals. All schools should take this seriously.

School factors can include problems with friendships, being bullied or problems with school work. There might be a fear of rejection, failure or embarrassment at school. There can be considerable pressure on children, both with the curriculum coverage and assessment with end of Key Stage (KS) testing. These KS tests (Standard Assessment Tests, SATs) can create pressure on teachers, parents and children and can cause anxiety for many. I have met many children and parents who were anxious because of these formal tests. Aside from the anxiety it generates, there are concerns that it may also lead to disengagement and dislike of education among children. The widespread grammar-school testing for the 11+ examination was abolished because it was perceived as unfair with potentially far-reaching implications for an individual's entire life. We can only speculate what the potential impact of the various Key Stage tests and streaming in secondary schools may have in the long-term.

Case History: Serena – Pain, But Not on Distraction

I saw Serena, a 6-year-old girl, with her father in a general practice surgery. Serena complained about 'always' having a 'tummy ache'. Once I had excluded any serious medical problems, I asked her about her favourite film. Serena's face lit up and she told me that she loves Disney films and started talking about some of her favourites. I continued to examine her abdomen (tummy) but now that Serena was distracted, she did not seem to feel any discomfort at all. This highlighted that perhaps there were other issues involved here. When I asked about school, Serena said she 'hated' the tests they must do and that they made her experience *tummy aches*. I encouraged her father to raise this with the teacher, who was receptive and helped to address Serena's anxieties and the tummy aches became less frequent.

How Can You Help Your Child with Anxiety?

The good news is that most children will grow out of much of their anxiety. However, some children will continue to be anxious and can be affected in adulthood, possibly developing depression. By identifying early if your child is anxious, you can help them promptly and may help prevent symptoms worsening or more serious problems developing later.

Some helpful practical tips to tackle anxiety

How to uncover problems and worries

- *Talk*. Be prepared to talk regularly to your child about any problems they may have.

- *Ask open questions*. If your child does not bring up a problem, consider doing so yourself. You need to be a detective! You know your children, but if you are concerned about them or their anxiety levels, start with open questions like, 'How are you feeling?' or 'How is everything at school?' Open questions are best, as they are non-intrusive and allow your child to speak freely without having thoughts or words put into their minds or mouths! However, if the *open* approach is persistently letting you down, you could probe a little more with a question like, 'You don't seem as happy as you usually are – is everything okay?' or 'You have seemed a bit quiet the last few days – has anything happened?' You may find it hard to have these conversations and if you do, or if you have not had any success, you could think of asking someone outside the immediate family (such as a grandparent, other relative or a good friend), whom both you and your child trust, to help. Only by talking about it can you delve into any underlying issues to be able to help your child.

- *Discuss options and strategies*. If you uncover an underlying concern, then talk to your child about possible strategies to overcome the problem. Try to encourage your child to think of possible solutions rather than dive in with your own ideas! This will help them to develop problem-solving strategies and may reduce future anxieties because they feel self-empowered and equipped to handle given situations. Discuss different options and then ask your child to choose the solution that they feel most comfortable with, so that they are in control and *own* it. Most importantly, do keep the dialogue going.

Explore children's anxieties and your own

- *Challenge negative thoughts.* Explore children's negative thoughts and foster alternative ways of thinking and more positive thoughts. Encourage a *have a go* mentality, which will help to develop their self-confidence and independence and reduce inner anxieties over time, by seeing that they can achieve whatever they set their mind to.

- *Avoid false reassurance.* Although it is tempting to always try to reassure your child about whatever they are anxious about, try to avoid doing so, as this may be false reassurance and it also does not foster an independent approach.

- *Modelling.* Be conscious of your own anxieties and responses and reactions to different situations. Children are great observers and may inadvertently copy behaviours. This is an example of *modelling* where children observe and copy behaviours. Try to be the person that you would like your child to become, so that they can learn, by observation and through your good example.

Practical strategies to deal with emotions

- *Verbalising.* Encourage your child to use words to describe emotions and when they feel them – such as *sad, unhappy, upset, angry, frustrated, annoyed, afraid* and, of course, *positive feelings* too! For younger children, drawing different feelings can work well too.

- *Fictional characters or other children.* If it is too difficult for your children to talk about their problems or emotions in depth, perhaps try relating the problem to someone else, whether that is a fictional character (for younger children) or a real child or adult.

- *Role play.* Try to prepare your child for specific events and potential emotions they may trigger by talking through situations or role playing in advance.

- *Possible triggers*. Think about whether your child might be anxious because of something happening in the home environment (such as arguing and conflicts with your partner, financial pressures or your own work or home stress) and try to address this, if possible.

- *Worry list*. Some families use a worry list or box.[3] This involves encouraging children to write down (you may need to do this for them if writing is difficult or becomes a chore) their worries in a list or place it in a box and you regularly look at them and discuss them. In turn, you ask the children not to think about their worries after they have written or 'posted' them until you discuss them together. The aim is to stop the day-long and perpetual worrying and anxiety which can occur and highlights that worries can be self-contained and managed. However, this strategy does not work so well for children who really struggle with the delay to address worries.

Spend quality time with your children

- *Quality time*. Spend quality time with your child – whether that is going to the shops, going for a walk or a scooter ride or playing a game. This may help them to feel more able to share emotional issues with you.

- *Shared mealtime(s)*. Have meals together regularly, if that is possible and practical. However, we fully appreciate that in many households across the country it would be a real luxury to be able to do this. So, perhaps, a regular weekend breakfast or other meal where the family comes together to discuss the past week and the following week and where you together talk about any problems for each family member. Perhaps rotate the order of who speaks each week. It helps children to know that grown-ups have problems too!

- *Routines*. Regular routines, particularly before bedtime, help provide children with a sense of boundaries and security and can help reduce anxieties about simple things.

- *Relaxation*. Try simple relaxation techniques together. Distractions and music can help too.

If you would like to find out more, do search the NHS Choices website on 'Anxiety in Children'.[2] This website discusses some useful strategies to help your child. If this is an issue that affects your child, please do read it.

Cognitive Behavioural Therapy (CBT) techniques may help your child if their problems are persistent and not responding to these strategies. The underlying principle of CBT is that how we think about things is associated with how we behave and feel. CBT is based on the idea that your child's thoughts, feelings and physical sensations are all interconnected and that their negative thoughts and feelings can trap them into a vicious cycle.[3,4] CBT is a complex concept and it is worth referring to the NHS Choices website to understand the principles. By using CBT, your child can unpick and change how they think about things, and therefore how they act. This, in turn, can change how they feel. It is important to encourage your child to think and consider different thoughts and ideas and adopt a *have a go* mentality by segmenting the actions into small 'steps'.[3,4] This can seem overwhelming and you may feel it is too much to handle alone. If you have tried all the above strategies and looked at the websites and still feel stuck, do consider talking to a healthcare professional. CBT does not help every situation or every child, so it is not suitable for everyone.

If any of the content here on stress and anxiety resonates, you may like to consider talking to your child's class teacher or someone in the school (such as a school nurse, if there is one), if you feel comfortable about doing so, or talk to a health professional at your general practice. Counselling, either offered through your child's school or through referral by your general practice, can be extremely helpful. There are Emotional Health Service organisations for children and, as mental health in children is currently a priority on the political agenda, the services that are available will hopefully proliferate and improve. Child and Adolescent Mental Health Services (CAMHS) offer help in diagnosis and support of mental health problems. There are also some very helpful (free) resources and organisations to help and support you and your family. These include the Young Minds parents' helpline and website,[5] Family Lives[6] helpline for parents and the Child Anxiety Network[7].

To help you start, here are a few simple, general questions, which can be very revealing and may help you to identify potential problems that need to be addressed.

What do you *like* about school? Is there anything you *dislike* about school?

What do you think you are *good* at? What do you find *difficult*?

At *school* and at *home*: What do you enjoy *doing*? What makes you *happy*? Does anything make you *sad or angry*? Does anything make you *worry*?

Over the years, we have observed that many individuals who have experienced adversities can find it easier to empathise with others' plights; furthermore, if these individuals have effectively overcome the adversities, it can help to make them stronger, more resilient and determined. These experiences and attributes may contribute towards developing better emotional intelligence (described in Chapter 2) and emotional resilience (described later in this chapter).

Dąbrowski's Overexcitabilities

Anxieties can also sometimes be triggered or aggravated by *overexcitabilities*, so they are worth thinking about.

Dąbrowski, a Polish psychologist, identified five areas in which individuals can exhibit intense behaviours.[8] These *overexcitabilities* form part of the *Theory of Positive Disintegration*, which Dąbrowski proposed in his book, *Positive Disintegration* on personality development. He uses the terms 'hyperexcitability', 'increased excitability', 'overexcitability' and 'excitability'. Dąbrowski proposes that increased excitability is a feature of high developmental potential together with special abilities and talents.

The five areas of *overexcitablity* which Dąbrowski discusses are: *psychomotor, mental (intellectual), sensual, imaginational* and *emotional*. Children with high ability and potential have been noted to have multiple areas of *overexcitabilities*, although, often, one of the five domains dominates. Consider looking up Dąbrowski's overexcitabilities on the internet. Carol Bainbridge has written an article based on Dąbrowski's overexcitabilities, which outlines, with examples, the different domains. I encourage you to read it, as it is accessible and engaging.[9]

Many parents I have shared these domains with, have found them fascinating. Do have a look and see if your child exhibits any of Dąbrowski's overexcitabilities.

Dąbrowski's Overexcitabilities[8]

Psychomotor excitability is common among highly able children and those with high potential and is characterised by high levels of energy. This may manifest as any of the following: fidgetiness, nervous tics or habits, rapid speech or compulsive talking, impulsiveness, competitiveness, sleeplessness and physical expression of emotions.

Mental (intellectual) excitability is one of the most widely recognised in highly able children and those with high potential. Children with this excitability demonstrate a highly active mind. These children may be constantly questioning their surroundings and what they are learning. Examples of characteristics for this domain include: deep concentration and an ability to maintain mental application, independent and analytical thinking, love of reading, and intense curiosity.

Sensual excitability is a hypersensitivity or heightened awareness to the five senses: sight, smell, taste, touch and hearing. For example, a child who dislikes certain sounds or noises, or smells or the sensation of certain clothes against their skin (such as clothing labels) or texture of certain foods. A child with a sensory excitability may have a particular appreciation of art, whether it is music, writing or other area.

Imaginative/imaginational excitability represents an intense fantasy life, which can even sometimes disrupt reality. It is an ability to use their imagination to project forwards to what might subsequently happen. This can be limiting for a child, as it can mean that they imagine worst-possible scenarios and it can inhibit them participating in different situations.

Emotional excitability represents some children with very strong emotions. Individuals with this excitability are sometimes the ones who people describe as: 'She [or he] is over-sensitive about everything.' Characteristics of this domain include anxiety, shyness, loneliness, concern, empathy for others, a need for comfort and security, feelings of inadequacy and inferiority, extreme emotions, a sense of responsibility or guilt, difficulties adjusting to changes, strong memories of feelings and a strong sense of fairness and justice.

Bullying – The Biggest Menace of this Century?

Twenty per cent of children and twelve per cent of adolescents report bullying at school, according to the Economic and Social Research Council (ESRC).

The Economic and Social Research Council (ESRC) is the UK's leading research and training agency addressing economic and social concerns. ESRC-funded research by Wolke and colleagues (2013, 2014, 2015) suggests that being bullied in childhood can be the cause of long-lasting and significant harm.[10,11,12] The authors report that victims are at greater risk of poorer health, weaker social relationships in adulthood and lower wealth. They recommend the need for more effective interventions to deal with bullying that could reduce long-term health and social costs for individuals and for society.

We hope your child has never been bullied and never will be, but it is helpful to be aware of this relatively common problem. If identified, bullying can be resolved, so that the victim is supported and the bully can be guided to understand his or her actions.

Bullying can be defined as unwanted, aggressive behaviour that involves real or perceived power imbalance. Both children who are bullied and those who bully can potentially experience long-term problems if the bullying is not addressed. Victims of bullying, especially if their self-confidence and self-esteem are destroyed, can also potentially become bullies themselves.

High ability and high performance can be a trigger for becoming a target for bullying. Bullying among children needs to be addressed as early as possible because a mindset can develop that bullying and causing distress is acceptable. We all know of examples of children and adults whose lives were severely affected because of persistent bullying – in workplace situations, teaching institutions and in social contexts.

Children who bully, use their power, whether that is physical strength or the use of embarrassing information or popularity over others, to exert control over or harm to others. The behaviour is typically repeated over time or has the potential to reoccur.

How Can You Identify Bullying?

There are three main types of bullying – verbal, physical and social bullying.

1. *Verbal bullying* involves saying or writing mean things. For example, it can involve name calling, teasing, taunting or threatening to cause harm.

2. *Physical bullying* involves hurting someone's body or possessions. It can include kicking, pinching, hitting, spitting, pushing, tripping, taking or breaking someone's things or making rude hand gestures in relation to another child.

3. *Social bullying* involves hurting someone's reputation or relationships. It can include deliberately excluding a child, telling other children not to be friends with someone, spreading rumours about someone or embarrassing a child in front of others. This includes 'cyberbullying'.

Bullying, unfortunately, can occur anywhere – within or outside school. Although more prevalent among secondary school children, cyberbullying is increasingly common and involves bullying via the use of social media. Cyberbullying can create as much emotional turmoil and negativity as any other type of bullying. The victim can lose confidence and self-esteem. The website Bullying UK covers the different types of cyberbullying that can occur and offers some practical advice on how to manage it.[13]

At What Age Can Bullying Start?

In the past, it was believed that bullying could only occur from school-age. However, there is increasing recognition that some children may start to bully others from a younger age. Whatever the age, targeted and repetitive verbal or physical acts can potentially have (long-term) damaging consequences for the recipient.

Case History: Mary

A bright child, Mary, was bullied at nursery – verbally and physically – over a period of time when aged 4 years old, by a child who was only a few months older. Among the many remarks was the comment, 'If you had white skin and brown hair like your daddy and not brown skin and black hair like your mummy, then I would like you' and 'You can't play princesses with us because you don't have white skin'. The bullying made an otherwise happy child, a sad, withdrawn and unhappy one and this continued for a long time, and made her dislike her skin and hair colouring, to the extent that she drew herself with white skin and blonde hair. The child who was very close to her grandmother repeatedly asked for her to tell her *sad stories*, perhaps a mechanism she used to make her feel better that there are other people who are unhappy too. Although there are still residual effects, due to the constant support at home, she is now happier and doing well. Her self-confidence also increased. The family had to work hard to understand what was happening and to help the child overcome the experience.

If a child is targeting another child with repeated physical or verbal insults, that may be described as bullying. It can be difficult to identify emergent bullying behaviour, but it is essential to do so, for the sake of the potential victim(s), perpetrator and beyond. Some degree of hitting, pinching or meanness, in a non-targeted manner, can be within normal development among preschool children. However, if it is targeted at one child or a small group of children, or if a child enjoys seeing another child hurt emotionally or physically, that causes concern. Bullies can deliberately and systematically work out ways to inflict emotional or physical harm and some may even laugh or are happy after they have done so and lack sensitivity and empathy. This may point to underlying problems in the perpetrators, such as family or social adversities, or child-specific problems, including learning difficulties, which need investigation and potential intervention.

Why are Children Bullied?

Children can be bullied for a variety of reasons. Examples include (perceived) high or low academic ability, appearance, race, religion, disability, home circumstances or being different in any other way. Essentially, anyone who is different from a bully, in some way, can become a potential target.

What are the Effects of Bullying?

Bullying is very destructive and can make victims feel awful about themselves and the world around them. It can affect a child's confidence, sense of security, happiness and overall wellbeing. Children may feel sad, lonely, possess low self-esteem and suffer from anxiety, fear and poor concentration. At the more extreme end, bullying can lead to self-harm, depression and suicidal thoughts. The aforementioned ESRC study, by Professor Wolke and his colleagues, suggested that bullying in childhood has a more detrimental impact than bullying received in adulthood (BBC News, 2013).[14] Another study showed the potential impact on subsequent *physical inflammation* and *functioning* in adulthood (Copeland *et al.*, 2014).[15]

As research has shown, bullying that occurs at school can be one of the strongest predictors of poor mental wellbeing. Sadly, research has also shown that children who were bullied tended to have lower Key Stage 1 SATs results and were also more likely to interact with children who are involved in antisocial activities (Gutman and Feinstein, 2008a).[16] Being a victim of bullying in the later primary school years has a strong relationship with lower achievement in secondary school (Gutman and Feinstein, 2008b).[17]

How Can You Manage Bullying?

It is important that if your child is being bullied, you seek help for them and for yourself – as it is just as challenging for a parent to witness their child being targeted. Every child should be able to feel happy in their (school) environment and you should be able to have the confidence and peace of mind to know that your child is not being bullied by anyone.

Here are a few practical tips for you to try if you think your child is affected by bullying:

- Keep away from any child or children who are involved in any type of bullying.
- Encourage your child to stay with children they feel safe with.
- Try not to reciprocate any bullying, as it may fuel further bullying.
- Keep an eye on what is happening and consider sharing it with the teacher, so they can understand the situation and offer help and support for your child.

- Ask the teacher what you can do in partnership to help your child.

- Share with your child that if another child says something mean to or about them, it usually reflects a lot about that child. Children (and adults for that matter) may say unkind things if they themselves feel insecure. Criticising others is a way of taking attention away from themselves and elevating their own sense of power and feeling of importance.

- Encourage assertiveness, which helps to deter bullies.

For more ideas, do read the NHS Choices website on bullying.[18]

Keeping in touch with the school is a very important part of bringing bullying to the attention of the school. However, depending on your school, you may want to think twice before using the word 'bullying', as it is a very sensitive topic. Instead, consider highlighting the facts and incidents and let the teachers deduce this for themselves. Most teachers are in their profession because they care about children, want them to be happy and will stop such behaviour, support the victim and help the perpetrator to identify and understand their wrongdoings.

Anti-bullying helplines provide advice and it is so much easier to manage these situations with support. Organisations include Childline,[19] Bullying UK[20] and Bullybusters[21].

On the other hand, if you think your child may be a bully (him or herself), it is equally important for you to seek help for them, so that the situation does not escalate and so that they can receive timely support. Do talk to your child's school.

How to Develop Assertiveness

Being assertive does not come easily, even for many adults. It does not equate to being rude. It is about *clever, smart communication*. It utilises being able to express thoughts and feelings honestly and potentially disagreeing with another person, but without being rude or offensive. Assertiveness comes under the premise that every child and adult has the right to say how they think and feel and has a right to fairness. The Children's Hospital of Pittsburgh has encapsulated some key messages for communication in their article on 'Assertiveness' on their website.[22] Assertiveness is an extremely useful skill to develop for many aspects of life in childhood and adulthood.

In relation to bullying, encourage your child to be or at least act confidently, as many bullies tend to prey on quieter or seemingly more vulnerable children. If a child is being mean to your child, perhaps consider encouraging your child to try showing *indifference*, to show that they are not bothered by the perpetrator's words or actions. I do acknowledge this is not easy for a child to do. Quite often a child who is bullied or been on the receiving end of cruel behaviour is more likely to be upset, tearful or display frustration through their behaviour. However, *if possible*, we should try to help our children to diminish the sense of power and control a bully feels and, therefore, the associated pleasure in putting someone else down.

An example of a conversation between a bully and a confident child.

Bully: You've got a funny nose.

Confident and assertive child: Mmm, maybe I do.

Bully: I said you've got a funny nose!

Confident and assertive child: Never mind, that's okay. I like it.

Bully: Idiot! (and walks off probably to find another potential target ...)

The strategy in this dialogue, between a bully and a confident, assertive child, works because the confident child is not rising to the insult and is not becoming upset or angry, which is usually the desired response that the bully is striving for. Agreeing with the bully or showing indifference, diffuses the situation and bores the perpetrator. You can practise role plays of different scenarios at home.

I will now outline emotional resilience, which is highly topical and is an attribute that can be learnt and developed.

What is Emotional Resilience?

Public Health England (PHE) describes emotional resilience as the capacity to *'bounce back'* from adversity (2014).[23] However, what does that mean in practice? A child who is emotionally resilient is typically able to overcome challenges and face adversity with confidence and with the ability to cope and move forward unscathed.

Being emotionally resilient means that, psychologically and emotionally, we can overcome difficult situations, and be able to cope with whatever life throws at us. However, many children (and adults) can feel helpless and hopeless when such challenges present themselves and do not feel able to overcome the adversity. Some of these children may develop a mental health issue, such as anxiety, depression, an eating disorder or addiction, as they grow older.

Resilience may not necessarily be an innate characteristic of a child's personality and the good news is that research has shown that resilience can be learnt and developed. Furthermore, the more resilient a child is, the happier and more successful they are likely to be. Being resilient can also enhance children's learning power because it contributes to positive mental wellbeing.

As PHE highlights (2014), resilience may contribute towards healthy behaviours, success, better employment and (positive) mental wellbeing, and a faster or more successful recovery from illness.[23] Professor Martin Seligman, an eminent US psychologist, supports the concept of improving children's *optimism*, as a way of enhancing children's resilience and wellbeing, reducing the risk of anxiety and depression and boosting school performance (Seligman, 2007).[24] The fact that you are reading this book shows how much you value your child's education and wellbeing, and that suggests you are already doing a significant amount to support your child.

You may be pleased to hear that the National Curriculum recommends regular *Personal, Social, Health and Economic* (PSHE) lessons for children across the age range. The *PSHE Association*,[25] funded by the Department for Education in England, highlights, in their guidance for teachers on 'Preparing to Teach About Mental Health and Emotional Wellbeing' (2015), that there are a few important factors that contribute towards emotional resilience and (positive) wellbeing.[26] This PSHE report presents the following factors that support (positive) emotional wellbeing and resilience:[26]

- *'Good communications skills*
- *Good problem-solving skills*
- *Healthy coping skills, including healthy responses to crisis events*
- *The knowledge, skills and confidence to seek help*

- *The ability to recognise, name, describe and understand a range of emotions*
- *Interaction, friends and social engagement*
- *Positive self-esteem and appreciation of difference and uniqueness*
- *The ability to manage difficult emotions in a healthy way*
- *Experience of, and ability to manage failure'*

The role of a parent is of paramount importance, so try to encourage and foster these factors cited in the PSHE report to boost your child's emotional resilience. You may wish to read this report and reflect on its content.

Happiness and Wellbeing

If we were to ask a class of children what they define as happiness, we would hear a range of different opinions. Depending on age, some children might say their birthday, a new bike, being rich, marrying a prince or princess, becoming famous or receiving presents. These are natural dreams and aspirations which children possess and we do not want to shatter them.

Some adults believe that people are born to be happy or unhappy and it is a fixed state in personality that cannot change. However, it is now recognised that there are strategies for all of us to become happier and live more fulfilled lives and that includes our children too. I have seen many children's lives transformed from those of hopelessness, with feelings of inadequacy or failure, to those of optimism and self-worth.

Happiness is a 'positive feeling' and we should all strive towards achieving it, for our children, our families and ourselves.

How Can You Help Cultivate a Happy Child?

Happiness transfers to those around you, especially your children. Therefore, start with yourself! Professor Sarah Stewart-Brown, a wellbeing expert at the University of Warwick, says *'feelings of contentment, enjoyment, confidence and engagement with the world are all part of [positive] mental wellbeing. Self-esteem and self-confidence are too'* (NHS Choices).[27] She continues by saying that although good mental wellbeing does not mean that you never experience negative feelings of situations you find difficult, it does help to feel you have the resilience to cope when challenges arise. She also highlights that (positive) wellbeing is something that needs to be worked on to achieve and requires action to develop.

The New Economics Foundation (NEF), in 2008, outlined five ways to improve an adult's wellbeing.[28] These five actions include: connect, be active, keep learning, take notice and give. The Children's Society, an English charity, worked with the NEF to see if these five domains for adults could be transferred to children to promote their wellbeing too.[29,30] Surveys and focus groups with children (aged 8–15 years) from six schools across the country showed that four of the five NEF actions (connect, be active, take notice and keep learning) work well for children. Although there was less evidence that 'giving', being kind and doing things to help others worked as well among children! However, the study discovered that creativity, imagination and play were important in promoting positive wellbeing for children.

So, think about incorporating these five elements highlighted by The Children's Society and NEF into your child's life:

- *Connect* – encourage your child to interact with those around them – family, friends and children inside and outside school.
- *Be active* – encourage your child to be active, whether that is in a playground or to take up a sport.
- *Keep learning* – provide opportunities to learn new skills that can help your child to gain more self-confidence. This might be riding a bike, baking a cake or learning to play an instrument.
- *Take notice* – be *mindful* – in a busy and stressful world, sadly even for children these days, try to encourage awareness in the here and now, in terms of surroundings, thoughts and feelings. This may help change the way your child feels about life and how he or she approaches challenges. This reflects *mindfulness*.
- *Be creative and play* – encourage your child to be artistic in its different forms – drawing or painting using different materials, making models, designing things, enjoying music, gardening and making up stories and plays.

Although it is not one of the listed five actions, it is still important to encourage your child to give to others, as the act of giving can help to foster kindness in your child.

Another important attribute to cultivate is humour. Having a good sense of humour is a great strength and asset. Try to see the funny side of situations and you will, hopefully, often be able to cope better. We know a family who, when they sit at the table, take turns to tell jokes or make up a new funny character, create funny accents and voices. According to the father, everybody laughs even at the most pathetic jokes. Perhaps try watching some *Mr Bean* sketches, which can appeal to younger and older children. I challenge you and your child not to laugh when you watch them!

The Great Outdoors

I was very engaged by an article, 'Play Outside! Twelve Ways to Health, Happiness, Intelligence, and Creativity, and to Environmental Sustainability' in Dona Matthews' blog (2014), in which she suggests that spending more time outdoors, preferably in natural settings, may be the simplest, healthiest and most economical remedy for the terrible increase in the numbers of children diagnosed with social, emotional and learning problems over the past two decades.[31]

Do consider encouraging your child to do some *gardening*, whether it is in a garden or planting seeds in a pot for a window sill, as it offers a wonderful opportunity for children to embrace nature and observe the changes that occur. An Ofsted schools' inspections report, in 2008, found that, *'when planned and implemented well, learning outside the classroom contributed significantly to raising standards and improving pupils' personal, social and emotional development'.*[32]

In summary, I have discussed anxiety and touched on the topic of depression, which is at the more severe end of this spectrum. I have covered emotional resilience, assertiveness and bullying, which may all be linked. Higher emotional resilience and assertiveness may help towards avoiding or managing bullying. Emotional resilience is fundamental for a child's happiness and success. Finally, I have highlighted the importance of 'happiness' and how you can help your child to be happier because, ultimately, a contented child is what every parent wants. A positive by-product of this, is that **a happy child is a happier learner than an unhappy child.** ☺

🔑 Key Points

- Anxiety is a common mental health problem in children.

- Twenty per cent of children and twelve per cent of adolescents report bullying at school.

- Dąbrowski described five *oversensitivities* in individuals, which are commonly observed among *'gifted'* children: psychomotor, mental (intellectual), sensory, imaginative and emotional. These oversensitivities can contribute to increased anxiety levels in children who possess them.

- Developing assertiveness may help to avoid bullying or enable it to be better managed.

- Help to encourage your child to develop emotional resilience, which is the capacity to bounce back from adversity.

- Five action points to help cultivate happiness in your child include: connect with family and friends inside and outside school; be physically active; keep learning new skills; take notice of the 'here and now' and appreciate surroundings; and finally, encourage creativity and play.

Chapter 8

HOW DOES FOOD AND PHYSICAL ACTIVITY HELP LEARNING AND WELLBEING?

Elizabeth Koshy

• •

Let us return to the question that I asked 90 parents: what they wanted most for their children. The answer was that they wanted their children to be happy, healthy and to do well in school and beyond. I think most parents would agree with this, as their desire for their child's future. This chapter focusses on the effect food and physical activity have on a child's health and wellbeing. A child who is hungry or has eaten too much sugary food may struggle to concentrate, which can affect learning. In Chapter 6, we considered Maslow's pyramid, which argues that *food and drink* are the first and most basic *need* that our bodies require before anything else can be achieved (Maslow, 1943).[1]

I will outline how eating the *right* foods can contribute to your child's health, energy levels and overall wellbeing, which, in turn, may help them to learn better and improve their performance. There are many myths and wrong information that circulate about food habits and how they affect children's learning. In fact, I have been asked many times: What does food have to do with nurturing and fulfilling potential, anyway? After reading this chapter, I hope you will see how important it is.

It is not only the food you eat which boosts your learning power. Physical activity also contributes to your child's general wellbeing. I will address both topics in this chapter.

This chapter is written with the appreciation that children do not always do what we recommend! However, adopting a *whole-family approach*, if possible, *may* offer the best chance of success.

Food and Wellbeing

You Are What You Eat

Well, there is a remarkable amount of truth in the saying, 'You are what you eat'. There has also been more media attention, in recent years, on the link between eating habits and health and wellbeing – for children and adults. A fit and healthy body can boost concentration and alertness, thus playing an important role in fulfilling children's potential in all aspects of their lives. Research has shown that children with healthy eating habits obtain the best from their body now and into adulthood. That does not mean your child can never have any *naughty* foods, like a chocolate bar, sweets or a slice of cake, or must look away every time they walk past a fast food outlet. Just remember to help your child keep the *naughty* foods in moderation and more as occasional treats, and you and they will not go far wrong. Sometimes it can be hard to convince children of the importance of adopting healthy food habits, and it can be so tempting to give in to demands for limitless sweets and junk food (as I know too well), but it is well worth trying to focus on both the short-term and long-term benefits for your child.

A balanced diet contributes to a stronger immune system, to help protect your child against common (infectious) illnesses, and potentially reduce the risk of frequent and prolonged absences from school. Taking care of what they eat may also improve their sleep patterns, energy levels, concentration and memory. These can all contribute to higher achievement and success in whichever field they show potential, whether it is sport, music, language or mathematics. By the way, there is little scientific evidence for old wives' tales that headstands raise a child's IQ by more than 20 points!

Many children and adults are overweight, and obesity levels have been increasing dramatically in recent decades. The National Child Measurement Programme (NCMP) measures the height and weight of about one million schoolchildren in England every year.[2] This provides a detailed picture of the prevalence of child obesity in this country. For 2015/16, 14% (about 1 in 7) of children in Year 6 (aged 10–11 years) were overweight and a further 20% (about 1 in 5) were obese. Among children in Reception (aged 4–5 years), 13% (about 1 in 8) were overweight and another 9% (1 in 11) were obese. This translates into over one third of 10–11 year olds and over one fifth of 4–5 year olds being overweight or obese in 2015/16. The World Health Organization (WHO) states that child and adult obesity, and its associated risks, have become of global concern.[3] I have met many children and young adults over the years who thought they were too young for any medical problems to affect them. If only this were true! However, let us be optimistic, as becoming overweight and obese is preventable, without starving.

What is the Body Mass Index (BMI)?

You can use a tool on the NHS Choices website to calculate your child's Body Mass Index (BMI) to see if their weight is within the recommended range for their age in relation to their height.[4] If your child's BMI is shown to be overweight or underweight using the BMI calculator, you should make an appointment at your general practice, to seek professional advice. It is important to intervene early to avoid future complications if your child is underweight (e.g. problems with bone density) or overweight (e.g. type 2 diabetes mellitus), as well as possible body image issues. If your child's BMI is too high or too low, do read the practical advice on the NHS Choices website and try to work with your child to implement changes. Modifying eating habits gradually, but consistently, does make a difference. Investigate the Change4Life website that covers this topic and gives practical advice on making positive changes.[5]

What Should Your Child Eat?

Healthy eating is about consuming a variety of foods, in the right quantities (to avoid excess calories leading to being overweight) to provide the necessary energy levels, macronutrients (carbohydrates, protein, fat and water) and micronutrients (vitamins and minerals) that your child's body requires to function optimally. It may all sound complex, but try to put this into practice gradually, so that it is not overwhelming for them (or you!). Remember, small changes make big differences.

The Eatwell Guide

Remember, your child's learning and fulfilment of potential are influenced by their general health and a healthy diet contributes to that. Public Health

England (PHE), a government agency, adopts and recommends the *Eatwell Guide* for adults and children aged over 2 years (PHE, 2016).[6,7] The guide is practical, easily accessible and shows how to build a healthy diet for children and adults. It includes a visual summary of the main food groups, represented as a plate of food. It shows different food groups and the role they should play in a healthy diet. I have included the key points and reproduced the image of the plate of food from the guide. I recommend that you download and use the *Eatwell Guide* booklet from the Government website. Consider putting a printout of the Eatwell Plate diagram on your fridge door to act as an *aide memoire*.[6,7] Remember to give children smaller plates and not adult-size plates, so as not to inadvertently encourage your child to over-eat.

Periodically, it can be fun to discuss family food habits and what your family eats, make lists and draw charts or pictures of what is eaten during a week and compare them with what is recommended in the *Eatwell Guide*.

The key points from the Eatwell Guide to adopt are as follows:[6,7]

- *Each day, aim to eat at least five portions of different fruits and vegetables.*
- *Incorporate starchy carbohydrates such as potatoes, bread, rice or pasta into meals. Where possible, use wholegrains, for example wholemeal bread or brown rice.*
- *Include dairy products in your diet. Otherwise dairy alternatives, such as soya products.*
- *Eat protein which may come in the form of beans, pulses, fish, eggs and meat.*
- *Aim to eat two portions of fish every week – one of which should be oily, such as salmon or mackerel, trout, herring or fresh tuna.*
- *Use unsaturated oils and spreads but only eat them in small amounts.*
- *Reduce intake of foods which are high in fat, salt and sugar, such as cakes and biscuits.*
- *Drink plenty of water.*

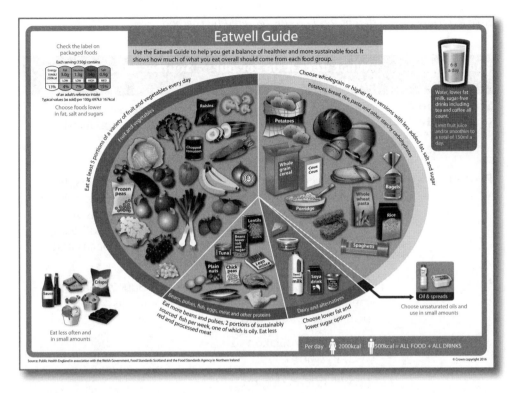

Figure 8.1 The Eatwell Guide. *Crown copyright, July 2016. Public Health England in association with the Welsh government, Food Standards Scotland and the Food Standards Agency in Northern Ireland.*[6,7]

Components of a Healthy Diet

If your children follow the Eatwell Guide, you will ensure that they take the seven main food groups which their bodies require: starchy foods (carbohydrates), protein, fats, minerals, vitamins, fibre and water. Have a glance at the different food groups in Table 8.1, which highlights their different functions, as well as potential sources.

Table 8.1 The seven different food groups required by the body.

Food group	What does it do for our bodies?	Sources in food
Starchy foods (carbohydrates)	Main source of energy and a range of nutrients in our diet: vitamins, iron, fibre and calcium	Bread, rice, potatoes and pasta (all preferably wholegrain)
Protein	Helps body to function, grow and repair (e.g. skin, hair and nails)	Eggs, dairy products, fish, meat, poultry (e.g. chicken and turkey), beans and pulses (e.g. baked beans, lentils, kidney beans and chickpeas)
Fats	Constituents of cell membranes. Contributes to healthy skin, heart and brain Energy and insulation to keep us warm ('Bad fats' can clog up arteries)	Dairy products, meat, nuts, seeds and oils
Minerals	Iron helps to make red blood cells which carries oxygen around the body Calcium is good for teeth and bones	Contained in lots of different foods, but especially fruits and vegetables Green vegetables (e.g. spinach) and red meat are good sources of iron
Vitamins	Help to keep body functioning and healthy Good for skin, nervous system, immune system, teeth and bones	Fruits and vegetables, dairy products (milk, eggs and butter) and some fortified breakfast cereals Vitamin D – primarily through exposure to sunlight
Fibre	Helps to digest your food and avoid constipation	Present in lots of different foods, including cereals and starchy foods, especially wholegrain varieties
Water	Needed for almost every process in your body	Water!

To supplement the table, below I have provided some additional information about fibre and water, as these are the two areas that I notice are frequently forgotten or overlooked. I have also included some information about the other groups in Appendix 2 (at the back of the book) for those of you who are interested in more detail.

Fibre

Fibre is important to aid your child's digestive system. It can typically be found in fruits, vegetables and wholegrain foods. A high fibre diet can reduce the chances of your child becoming constipated, which can be very unpleasant. In the longer-term, into adulthood, a high fibre diet *may* also help towards preventing heart disease, type 2 diabetes mellitus, weight gain and some cancers, including bowel cancer (Bradbury et al., 2014).[8]

Case History: Sam, 7 years old

Late afternoon one day, Sam's mother brought him to the surgery with long-standing abdominal pain ('tummy aches'). After excluding serious medical and emotional problems by talking to Sam and his mother, and examining him, the following conversation took place:

Elizabeth: Sam, tell me what you ate today?

Sam: I had a chocolate bar and a packet of crisps for breakfast.

Elizabeth: Do you have school lunches?

Sam: No, don't like them, they are boring.

Elizabeth: So, what did you have for lunch?

Sam: I had packed lunch with lots of treats.

Elizabeth: Tell me what was in your packed lunch.

Sam: A bottle of lemonade, a jam sandwich, a packet of salt and vinegar crisps and a chocolate bar.

Elizabeth: And what will you be eating this evening?

Sam: My favourite – sausages and chips with lots of tomato sauce and chocolate cake for pudding.

Elizabeth: Do you eat fruits and vegetables?

Sam: No, they taste yuck!

I asked Sam and his mother, specifically, about foods that are high in fibre, such as wholegrain bread, pasta, rice and fruits and vegetables, and discovered that Sam ate very few of these foods. Therefore, the low fibre diet seemed likely to have contributed to constipation and the 'tummy aches', as he only passed motions infrequently and with considerable difficulty and discomfort.

Sam's mother had come for a prescription. Instead, I suggested that she should try to give Sam foods that are high in fibre and encourage him to drink plenty of water for two weeks and to return for a follow-up appointment. This had a happy ending. The 'tummy aches' disappeared and Sam brought photos on his mother's phone of all the 'healthy' foods he had been eating.

Water

Sufficient water intake is critical for survival. Hydration refers to drinking sufficient fluids for the body. Although adults can drink fluids when they want, children typically depend on caregivers for food and drink (D'Anci *et al.*, 2006).[9] Children have a higher percentage of body water than adults and also have different thirst sensitivities to adults. Children are at greater risk of dehydration than adults because of their larger surface area to mass ratio. Right, that's the pure science over!

Dehydration can lead to some of the following symptoms: thirst, tiredness, difficulty concentrating, reduced alertness, headaches, dry cough, dry mouth and bad breath, dry eyes, dizziness and tummy problems. As dehydration can affect concentration, attention and memory, it can adversely affect learning in the classroom. This is particularly important during the warm summer months. Well-hydrated pupils may concentrate better, as they are less distracted by the symptoms of dehydration, such as tiredness, thirst and irritability. It can therefore lead to better behaviour in the classrooms and help the children and their teachers!

From my experience of talking to parents and children, over the years, I have noticed that children of all ages are notoriously poor at drinking water and keeping well-hydrated. Research studies support this observation of large numbers of children being (at least) mildly dehydrated both in hot and cold climates (Bar-David *et al.*, 2005[10] and Fadda *et al.*, 2012[11]). Several studies have shown that adults may experience detrimental effects on their cognitive functioning with dehydration. Evidence is emerging that children are adversely affected too (Edmonds and Burford, 2009[12]; Shirreffs *et al.*, 2004[13] and Fadda *et al.*, 2012[11]).

There has been a proliferation of sugary drinks that appeal to many children. As many health experts warn us, not only are these drinks bad for children's teeth, by damaging the tooth enamel, they also increase the likelihood of them becoming overweight or obese, as many contain a lot of sugar and calories. The introduction of the *Sugar Tax* by the Government in 2016, raised awareness among all of us surrounding the perils of consuming sugary drinks (BBC News, 2016).[14]

Water is the ideal drink for children to have at any time of the day; it does not contain natural or added sugars, artificial sweeteners, caffeine or additives. Drinking sufficient water can also help towards avoiding problems with the urinary tract, such as urinary tract infections and bowel problems, such as constipation.

Since January 2015, the Government, through the *School Food Plan*, recommended that drinking water must always be readily available on school premises in England.[15] This is a welcome addition and we need to actively encourage children to make use of it. Many schools actively encourage children to bring a full water bottle to school every day, which is very helpful, as it also provides an indicator to parents of how much their child drinks during the day. If your child takes a bottle to school, do not forget to ask about or check the water level after they return from school!

How Much Should Children Drink?

Although there are no consistent guidelines, surrounding how much children should drink, there are some facts we do know from research. Fluid requirements depend on many factors including age, sex of child, levels of physical activity, climate and environmental temperature.

The European Food Safety Authority (EFSA, 2010) recommends the following water intake requirements: 1.1–1.3 litres/day for boys and girls aged 4–8 years, 1.3–1.5 litres/day for girls aged 9–13 years and 1.5–1.7 litres/day for boys 9–13 years.[16] Children are generally advised to have about 6–8 glasses (or cups) of fluid a day, depending on the size of the drinking container (in addition to the water naturally contained within the food consumed within their diet). Younger children generally have relatively small drink measures and older children need larger drink measures. These quoted quantities are regarded as appropriate levels for conditions of moderate environmental temperature and moderate physical activity levels. If you are unsure about how much these volumes of fluid represent, try filling an empty bottle which shows its capacity (how much it holds) using your child's drinking glass or cup. You can involve your child in this activity to give them a greater understanding.

If your child is accustomed to consuming sugary drinks it may take a while to adjust to drinking water, but it can be done although it may take a little (or a lot) of patience and perseverance from them (and you!)

Additional Aspects of Diet

Vegetarians and vegans

If your child is a vegetarian or vegan, it is important for them to acquire their protein and iron from alternative sources, such as nuts, breakfast cereals fortified with iron, dark green leafy vegetables (such as broccoli) Quorn™, lentils, beans, tofu, and eggs (if not vegan). Dried fruit (such as apricots and prunes) also help towards a balanced and healthy diet.

Superfoods

There has been considerable media attention surrounding *superfoods* during recent years. These so-called superfoods include those that are high in antioxidants (such as vitamins A, C and E, selenium and beta-carotene) and omega-3. Antioxidants are chemicals which are believed to help protect our body from the harmful effects of *free radicals*. Free radicals are chemicals naturally produced in the cells (within our bodies) that can cause cell damage. Examples of superfoods include spinach, broccoli, beetroot, garlic, blueberries, pomegranates and goji berries. However, there are mixed research findings surrounding their potential health benefits and some of the superfoods are very expensive (NHS Choices). However, eating foods such as spinach and broccoli contribute to our fruit and vegetable intake, and, if there are additional health benefits, which have not yet been fully established, then even better!

The Mediterranean Diet

When I asked some teenagers if they knew what a Mediterranean diet means, one child jokingly stated that you eat it on the plane travelling to Mediterranean countries.

Seriously, however, this diet adopts the traditional, healthy habits of those who live in countries bordering the Mediterranean Sea, including France, Italy, Greece and Spain. It consists of lots of fruits, vegetables, beans, cereals and wholegrain foods, including bread, rice and pasta. There is also fish, white meat, smaller quantities of red meat and the use of unsaturated fats, such as olive oil, rather than saturated fats (e.g. butter). Oily fish, which is part of the Mediterranean diet, is a good source of protein, some B vitamins, selenium and vitamin D. The proportions of the different food types in this diet reflect those within the *Eatwell Guide*, which can promote a good, balanced diet for children and adults.

Furthermore, eating at least five portions of fruits and vegetables a day may also lower the chances of heart disease, stroke and some cancers in adulthood (Martínez-González *et al.*, 2015).[17] Although it is extremely rare for children to suffer from heart disease, this highlights how important the Mediterranean diet is for your whole family to adopt earlier rather than later.

Why not try making a list of the different food items from the Mediterranean diet your family consumes and perhaps use it as an opportunity for a geography lesson to find out where these foods typically originate?

Continues on next page…

Continued from previous page…

Another useful strategy is to create a weekly meal plan and try to include the different food groups, in the right quantities, in your family meals. This way, you can work out the week's meals in advance. You can search the Change4Life website for some recipe ideas for healthy, balanced meals. You can discuss the different meal options with your child, choose the ingredients in the shop (or online) together. Cooking together can also help.

All of this can also be educational!

Omega-3 and Other Polyunsaturated Fatty Acids

You may have heard about some of the discussions on the virtues of the polyunsaturated fatty acids (PUFAs), for example, in oily fish, being good for health and wellbeing (NHS Choices).[18] There are two main PUFAs – omega-3 and omega-6. Omega-6 is typically found in vegetable oils, including sunflower and rapeseed oils, as well as some nuts. Omega-3 is found in oily fish (such as salmon, fresh tuna, trout, sardines, mackerel, kipper and herring), as well as some nuts and seeds, and eggs.

There has been much media attention specifically surrounding omega-3 because, unlike omega-6, our diets are typically low in omega-3. Omega-3 fatty acids are long-chain PUFAs which must be obtained from the diet. They are essential fatty acids, required by every cell membrane (wall) in our bodies and are thought to have some potential additional benefits that are still being researched (NHS Choices).[18] If you are interested in this topic, I have included more information on this area in Appendix 2.

Nutrition Labels on Food

I know of parents and children who have developed an interest in demystifying the *traffic light* food nutrition labels at the supermarket and had fun doing this. Let me explain. Consider using the traffic light food labels to guide you and your family towards healthier options (check some of the food packages at home and the examples on the NHS Choices website).[19] The colours indicate *high* (red), *medium* (amber) and *low* (green) levels of energy, fat, saturated fat, sugar and salt. Aim for foods with more greens and ambers and fewer red labels. Remember, restricting saturated fats may help towards reducing the likelihood of developing high cholesterol levels, heart disease and strokes in adulthood. High sugar content is bad for your child's teeth and can represent excess calories, which may lead to unwanted extra weight gain. High salt intake can lead to an increase in blood pressure, particularly when older, which can, in turn, increase the risk of developing heart disease and having a stroke. Sorry to be depressing! Your child, like most children, may think they are young and invincible and have a very long life ahead of them, but if they start to adopt healthy habits while they are young, you can tell them that they might be even healthier and live even longer! Additionally, it may be easier for them to adjust their taste buds to a diet which is low in sugar, fat and salt while they are young, as so often in life it is easier and better to adopt good habits early! However, the world seems so *unfair* that some of the tastiest foods seem to come with a *red* warning!

Sugar Intake

The World Health Organization (WHO) recommends that children and adults should reduce their daily intake of *free* sugars to less than 10% of their total energy intake (WHO, 2014).[20] The WHO also states that a further reduction to below 5% per day would provide additional health benefits.

Your child should aim to have only small quantities of foods with high sugar content. Ideally, they should swap them for healthier alternatives or keep them for occasional treats. Suggested healthy snacks to substitute include: fruit, vegetable sticks (e.g. carrots, cucumber and celery), wholemeal pitta bread with hummus, yogurt, breadsticks, rice cakes and savoury crackers with cheese. These can taste delicious, as well as contribute to good health. I know from experience, as a mother and doctor, how incredibly difficult substituting can be. However, all we can do is patiently try to do our best!

Breakfast

Breakfast, like other meals, provides glucose, the fuel for children to function physically and mentally. Glucose is the major source of energy for the central nervous system, including brain functioning.

Adults who are regular breakfast eaters tend to adopt healthier lifestyle behaviours and have healthier body weights compared with those who skip breakfast (de la Hunty and Ashwell, 2006).[21] Children who regularly eat breakfast similarly tend to be less likely to be overweight than those who eat breakfast less frequently (Hansen and Joshi, 2008).[22] Furthermore, children who eat breakfast appear more likely to meet nutritional intake guidelines than those who skip breakfast. Unfortunately, the proportion of children eating breakfast in the UK has fallen over the years, alongside the nutrient quality of the breakfast consumed.

The UK government acknowledged and addressed the widespread research and media interest in the possible impact of skipping versus consuming breakfast on aspects of learning and memory by commissioning the report 'Breakfast and Cognition: A literature review' (Public Health England, 2013).[23] Overall, the research studies quoted in this review found that having breakfast compared with skipping breakfast can benefit memory and aspects of brain functioning, although it is still not clear which cognitive domains it may help and it may depend on the type of assessment utilised.[23] There is ongoing research investigating the potential relationship between specific breakfast composition and different learning and behavioural outcomes, and particularly longer-term attainment. However, in the meantime, try to encourage your child to have a nutritious daily breakfast!

Recently, Public Health England (PHE) reported that children are consuming large quantities of sugar within their breakfasts, which can represent half their daily allowance even before they start the school day (PHE, 2017;[24] BBC News, 2017[25]). PHE raised concerns about the quantity of sugar in cereals, juices and spreads consumed at breakfast time. The National Diet and Nutrition Survey found that 4–10 year olds were eating double the amount of sugar than maximum limits recommended for their age groups. For those of you who like your smartphone applications, PHE recommends using the Change4Life 'Be Food Smart' App, which enables you to scan food package barcodes to find out the sugar content of your meal.[26] Your children are likely to be fascinated by this and, because it's immediate and visual, it can make a real difference!

As part of the School Food Plan, the Department for Education awarded a contract to 'Magic Breakfast' to organise breakfast clubs for schools where over 35% of pupils are eligible for free school meals and where there was no existing breakfast provision.[27] This does raise a question in my mind – what about schools with less than 35% eligible pupils – what happens to those with, for example, 30% of children on free school meals? Research shows that children from poorer backgrounds may be the ones who are most likely to benefit from breakfast and such food interventions (Street and Kenway, 1999[28]; Ells *et al.*, 2008[29] and Edefonti *et al.*, 2014[30]). Although, as these studies highlight, it remains unclear whether the advantage of breakfast clubs stems from the meals themselves, the increased school attendance or other factors.[28,29,30]

Intuitively, the consumption of a nutritious, lower-sugar content, slow-energy releasing breakfast is likely to be most advantageous, although the exact details surrounding the composition remain unclear.

Case History: Suma

I vividly remember a winter morning when Suma (8 years old) was brought by her aunt to see me when I was working in a general practice in a deprived part of London.

The family was concerned by Suma's teacher mentioning that she was often falling asleep late morning and might be missing valuable learning. I first needed to rule out any serious medical or social issues, or sleep-related problems. Trying to relate the significance of repeatedly falling asleep late morning, I asked Suma what she ate for breakfast. Suma was quick to tell me how much she loved her breakfast and that she had a different flavour ice cream every morning with a strawberry milkshake. Her aunt told me that they tried to hide the ice cream, under other frozen foods, but she always managed to find it.

I told Suma and her aunt to try to change her breakfast and gave her some suggestions (including brown bread and an egg on some days and on other days to have wheat flakes with her favourite fruits).

When Suma returned, with her mother this time, Suma asked if I can do 'magic', because she hadn't fallen asleep once and, instead, she had become a class chatterbox during this time. We had a long discussion on the importance of eating the right foods, particularly the need for slow-energy releasing breakfasts. A few months later, when she came with a bruised knee, I asked them how the morning tiredness had been and was told she was obtaining higher marks for mental maths. This was a pleasing outcome.

There are still many questions surrounding the potential effects of different elements of diet on educational attainment. However, there is overwhelming evidence on the health benefits of a balanced diet. The ideal diet should be low in fat, sugar and salt and high in vegetables and fruits and include slow-energy releasing carbohydrates. In addition, you should promote physical activity. Together they can help to reduce the likelihood of being overweight or obese with associated medical conditions (Ells, 2008).[29] Therefore, perhaps this should be a focus for parents?

Physical Activity and Wellbeing

Again, returning to the theme of parents aspiring for their children to be healthy, happy and doing well in school, the role of physical activity in achieving this is of paramount importance.

What is Physical Activity?

The World Health Organization (WHO) defines physical activity as: *'any bodily movement produced by skeletal muscles that requires energy expenditure'*. Furthermore, the WHO highlights that, *'physical inactivity has been identified as the fourth leading risk factor for global mortality [deaths] causing an estimated 3.2 million deaths globally'*.[31]

As the National Institute for Health and Care Excellence (NICE, 2009) highlights, physical activity includes everyday activity, such as walking or cycling to travel from one destination to another.[32] Physical activity of moderate intensity, pursued on a regular basis, has significant benefits for health. It may help to reduce the risk of developing heart disease, type 2 diabetes mellitus, colon and breast cancer, as well as depression. Additional benefits include reducing the likelihood of hip or vertebral (spine) fractures and help to control body weight. These conditions typically affect adults, although unfortunately type 2 diabetes and depression have increasingly affected children in recent decades. Importantly, lifestyle modifications in childhood can help to develop healthier habits into adulthood. NHS Choices discusses physical activity in children and has produced a helpful information sheet.[33]

The term *physical activity* should not be confused with *exercise*, which is a subcategory of physical activity that is planned, structured, repetitive and aims to improve or maintain one or more components of physical fitness. Both moderate and vigorous intensity physical activity can bring health benefits.

How Much Physical Activity Should Children Undertake?

The World Health Organization (WHO) recommends children and adolescents aged 5–17 years undertake the following, unless there are specific reasons not to:[31]

- *'At least 60 minutes of moderate to vigorous intensity physical activity daily.*
- *Physical activity of more than 60 minutes daily will provide additional health benefits.*
- *Most of the physical activity should be aerobic. Activities should include those that strengthen muscle and bone, at least three times per week.'*

The target of 60 minutes daily can be accumulated in shorter bouts spread out through the day, so it does not have to be one long stint of 60 minutes in one go.

What Type of Physical Activities Should Children Undertake?

Moderate intensity activity increases breathing and heart rates to a level where you can feel your pulse and feel warmer. It might make a child sweat on a hot or humid day, or when indoors. Vigorous activity makes you feel out of breath and/or sweat. Research has shown that 1 minute of vigorous activity is about the equivalent to 2 minutes of moderate activity.

Examples of *moderate* physical activity include playing in the playground, walking to school, rollerblading, skateboarding and cycling on relatively level ground.

Examples of *vigorous* physical activity include swimming, running, football, rugby, energetic dancing, gymnastics, cycling fast or in a hilly area or martial arts.

School Physical Education (PE) lessons can fit under moderate or vigorous categories, depending on the type of activity undertaken.

So, perhaps talk to your child about different (new) physical activities to explore.

Why Undertake Physical Activity?

As the National Institute for Health and Care Excellence (NICE) highlights (2009), appropriate levels of physical activity contribute to the development of:[32]

- *'healthy bones, muscles and joints;*
- *healthy heart and lungs;*
- *better co-ordination and movement control;*
- *easier maintenance of a healthy body weight'.*

The NHS Choices website highlights that vigorous activity can result in better general health, stronger muscles and bones and higher self-confidence levels.[33] This can, in turn, contribute to higher performance in academic and non-academic pursuits and overall wellbeing.

The Public Health England (PHE) report, in 2014, 'The link between pupil health and wellbeing and attainment' highlighted that there is a positive association between physical activity levels of children and academic attainment.[34] A UK study found that the amount of moderate to vigorous physical activity with which pupils aged 11 years engaged with had an effect on academic performance for maths, English and science at 11, 13 and final GCSE exam results (Booth *et al.*, 2014).[35] So, try to encourage your child to embrace physical activity!

The release of certain chemicals in our brains can make us feel happy. Physical activity can increase the production of some of these chemicals (including endorphins). The Royal College of Psychiatrists highlights that physical activity may have potential psychological benefits and can help with symptoms of anxiety and depression.[36] Furthermore, participating in physical activity can assist in children's social development and provide opportunities for confidence building and adopting healthy behaviours, which may help them steer away from tobacco, alcohol and drug use in future years and perform better academically at school.

There is also a type of physical activity referred to as *Non-Exercise Activity Thermogenesis* (NEAT). This represents the energy used daily that does not include sleeping, eating or sports-like exercise (Levine, 2002;[37] Levine *et al.,* 2006[38]). It includes the energy used for walking to school and fidgeting! We may not realise it, but even trivial activities increase metabolic rate and it is the cumulative impact of different actions that culminate in an individual's daily NEAT levels. So, when you see your child fidgeting and, perhaps, feel a little frustrated and think or say 'keep still!' or 'not again!' just remember they are increasing their NEAT levels, which is contributing to their fitness and wellbeing!

Key Points

- Healthy eating means eating the right foods in the appropriate quantities, according to the *Eatwell Guide* and avoiding the wrong foods or at least eating them in moderation.

- Try to incorporate the *Mediterranean diet* into your child's daily life.

- Remind your child to drink plenty – ideally water – during the day to keep well-hydrated.

- Encourage your child to have a daily breakfast (not high in sugar) that releases energy slowly over the morning.

- Physical activity can contribute towards improved school performance, mood, self-confidence, social development and overall health.

- Encourage your child to increase their *NEAT* levels, which is the energy used daily that does not include sleeping, eating or sports-like exercise.

Part III: Conclusions

Chapter 9

FINAL THOUGHTS

Valsa Koshy and Elizabeth Koshy

· ·

We hope that you have found reading our book interesting and useful. This would not have been possible without the help and support of parents who had read and commented on the content. Our aims in writing this book are twofold: to support parents to understand the different views and perspectives on what constitutes giftedness; and for them to adopt the simple, practical strategies we suggest. Our message is that it is time to move away from labelling children as gifted and, thereby, creating a non-gifted group. Parents and teachers should focus on what children's special aptitudes or gifts are, and nurture them. Children possess different abilities and interests and, as parents, we are in an ideal position to observe their passions and encourage them to develop those. By doing this, we will be identifying the talents of individuals, which will make our world a better place. By working with schools, parents can make a real difference to their child's talent development.

We also believe that positive wellbeing – both mental and physical – is of paramount importance for children to realise their full potential. Every day, we all hear from other parents and the media about various aspects of children's health and what we should and should not be doing. We have brought many of the key messages on mental health, good food habits and physical activity, together in Part II of the book, highlighting research, policies and some common sense.

We hope you enjoy spending quality time with your children – talking, thinking, reading and laughing together.

Answers to the Questions Posed in the 'Parent Conversations' Section

At the beginning of this book in the Parent Conversations section, we referred to questions we have frequently been asked by parents. We promised to provide our answers at the end of the book. Here they are:

Q1: *I am not all that familiar with terms like giftedness, talent, very able and so on. If I don't know these, how can I tell if my child is gifted?*

A: You are not alone in this. There are no definitions, or agreements among experts or among lay people, of what these terms mean. These words can have different meanings for different people. Chapter 2 describes the many different views and perspectives, but regardless of the terminology used, it is worth you investing in finding out how to spot your child's special gifts and develop them.

Some people refer to gifted children as those who score highly in intelligence tests or academic examination assessment. A world renowned and highly respected expert – Professor Howard Gardner from Harvard University – has developed the now widely accepted theory on Multiple Intelligences that tells us that children can be gifted in different areas (Chapters 2 and 3).

Q2: *My friend's child came home with a letter from school saying she is gifted. My son scores much higher marks than this child in mathematics and yet, I didn't get a letter.*

A: In 1999, government policy recommended that schools in England select their Gifted and Talented (G&T) children and meet their needs. Although the policy was discontinued in 2010, some schools still select such a group and inform the parents. Other schools decided not to do this. Working with schools and teachers, this was a topic which we explored in some depth and found that schools which decided not to tell their parents did so, because they found it difficult to describe some children as G&T, and others not. The difficulty lies in the fact that children have different abilities, strengths and interests. It is possible to identify these special strengths and, if a child shows unusual capability or achievement in particular areas much higher than that expected for a child at that age, he or she may be described as gifted or talented in that area. In fact, in schools where they followed this way of identifying special gifts, teachers felt able to tell the parents what their children were gifted in. What is even more important is that parents and teachers then worked together to nurture and develop these gifts (Chapters 2 and 3).

Therefore, we encourage you to ask, 'What are my child's gifts?' rather than, 'Is my child gifted?' Ideally, the triad of children, teachers and parents can then work towards the same goal and make sure that all gifts and talents are nurtured from a young age.

Q3: *My daughter is very disruptive in class, but we find her extremely bright and she responds to challenges at home. What is wrong?*

A: Perhaps you could go and talk to her teacher and see if she has any ideas on why your daughter might be misbehaving and delve deeper into this issue. It is very rare for a teacher to resent parents sharing their concerns or information about what children's particular interests are, but just remember to do this in a sensible and sensitive manner. Valsa works with hundreds of teachers and her advice is not to challenge or confront a teacher with: *My child is gifted, but she is bored with the lessons.* (Chapters 4 and 5).

Q4: *Our 6-year-old boy is at least 4 years ahead of the others in his class in mathematics. Why can't the school move him to a class of older children?*

A: As highlighted in Chapter 5, the process of moving children so that they can work with older children is often described as *acceleration*. Although it is possible to do that, many of the parents we have worked with have not found this an overall positive solution. It can work well sometimes, but quite often children have the ability to understand complex ideas and do well in terms of achievement scores, but they lack the emotional maturity to make friendships with an older age group. This has, in some cases, led to teasing and bullying (Chapters 3 and 5).

Q5: *I am often told I must praise my child whenever I can. Recently, I read somewhere that it is not good to just praise children and that I should challenge them.*

A: Praising children for their achievement and efforts is absolutely necessary for their self-esteem and development. However, Professor Carol Dweck, from Stanford University, says we need to balance the praise with challenge. She maintains that children need to aspire higher and take risks rather than be complacent that they are doing the best they can. You could respond with: *That is good Josh. How well do you think you have done?* Is there a more challenging question you can think of or ask a question starting with: *What if...?* and suggest a new way to look at a situation (Chapters 1 and 5).

Q6: *My son is gifted. He is a loner and is very unhappy. He tells me he has no friends. What should I do?*

A: You should let the child's teacher know and discuss this with the school. Children can be unhappy for all sorts of reasons. Your son could have interests or ideas which may not fit in with his peers and he may feel uncomfortable about it. It may be that he has very high expectations of himself and his work may not be reaching the perfection he aims for. There may also be issues surrounding his emotions that are affecting him. Chapters 6 and 7 cover some areas to consider. Teachers have a range of effective ideas to address loneliness and unhappiness among children. Making your son work with a partner – perhaps of a similar ability or interests – or giving him a responsibility in a group task where his abilities enhance the group's achievement can work successfully (Chapters 6 and 7).

Q7: *I keep hearing about helping children to think. What is that and how do you do that? Isn't that what the school is supposed to do?*

A: Schools are offering more and more opportunities to help children to think and reflect. Parents can help in a number of ways during the course of the day and while involved in day-to-day activities like reading, watching television and using the internet. We have seen children developing efficient general strategies and solving logic problems; they seem to be able to transfer and apply these strategies to school work, examinations and real life. Read Chapters 4 and 5 which give a number of ideas parents have used and positively shared their experiences with us (Chapters 4 and 5).

Q8: *We are a poor family. Neither my husband nor I had a proper education. We left school before we were 16. Are there things we can do to help our daughter, so we can make sure she has better opportunities?*

A: There is no reason why parents who have not had higher education or a university degree should not encourage their children's gifts and talents to be developed. Many parents in similar situations have told us that they want their children to do better than they did themselves. We have run university programmes, which have been very successful in achieving this. There is no evidence that learning capabilities are lower in any part of the community. It is often a case of denied opportunities or parents not knowing how to make the most of opportunities. Most universities provide support for parents like you (Chapters 1, 3, 4 and 5).

Q9: *You often see gifted children being arrogant and looking down on their teachers and peers. Is this always the case?*

A: There is no evidence that gifted children are automatically arrogant or that they *look down* on their teachers. Although some children start feeling superior when they become aware that they are labelled as gifted, and may, as a result, behave differently, our overwhelming experience has been that children with exceptional gifts or talents often have a high degree of humility, empathy and a strong sense of justice (Chapter 3).

Q10: *Are there any checklists I can use to help me decide if my child is gifted?*

A: There are many checklists available and these are interesting and very useful to reflect on. Children do not fit into checklists, as they are unique individuals. However, some characteristics listed in checklists encourage us to be aware of and reflect on what may be displayed by different children. We have included checklists in Chapter 3; the one based on Howard Gardner's MI theory is particularly useful (Chapter 3).

Q11: *Is it good or bad for children to be labelled gifted?*

A: Our own research suggests that many teachers feel uncomfortable in creating G&T lists. The whole concept of giftedness is complex and in our view labelling is counterproductive. Research conducted in the USA, by Professor Carol Dweck, suggests that labelling children as gifted may lead to them giving up on challenges for fear of failure (Chapters 1, 3 and 5).

Q12: *Does a child have to be gifted and talented in all subjects to be considered a 'gifted child'?*

A: It is highly unusual for a child to be gifted in all subjects. Typically, a child has one or two particular gifts, for example, in mathematics and music, or sport and art. If you consider the Nobel Prize winners, their talents are in specific areas, such as Physics, Economics and Literature. So, individuals who excel usually only do so in one or two particular fields (Chapters 2 and 3).

*   *   *

At the beginning of the book, we acknowledged that we fully appreciate how difficult it can be for parents, carers and grandparents to translate knowledge and theory into practice with children. However, if you take note of *some* of the ideas we have provided in this book, you can at least *try* to put some of them into practice. At the end of the day, all we can strive for is to do our best for our children. Good luck with the journey!

References

In the following pages, we have included references to books and articles, as well as websites which readers may wish to refer to and explore further. These are presented in the order that they appear in each of the chapters, for ease of reference. Some references, therefore, are repeated under different chapters.

Introduction

1) United States Congress 1972 (P.L. 95–561, Title IX, Part A, Section 901) http://www.usd383.org/Home/ShowDocument?id=7878 (accessed 28th February 2017).

2) Desforges, C. and Abouchaar, A. (2003) *The Impact of Parental Involvement, Parental Support and Family Education on Pupil Achievements and Adjustment: A Literature Review (Report 433)*. London: Department for Educations and Skills. This is one of the most influential and quoted studies on the role of parents in supporting their children's education.

Part I: Nurturing Children's Gifts

Chapter 1

1) National Association for Gifted Children (NAGC) in the United States of America (USA) https://www.nagc.org/ (accessed 4th July 2017).

2) Terman, L.M. (1925) *Genetic Studies of Genius, Volume 1: Mental and Physical Traits of a Thousand Gifted Children*. Stanford: Stanford University Press.

3) Department for Education and Employment (1999) *Excellence in Cities*. London: Department for Education and Employment.

4) Department for Children, Schools and Families (2008) *Identifying Gifted and Talented Learners – Getting Started*. London: Department for Children, Schools and Families (DCSF).

5) Sternberg, R. and Ambrose, A. (2016) *Giftedness and Talent in the 21st Century*. The Netherlands: Sense Publications.

6) Koshy, V., Mitchell, C. and Williams, M. (2006) *Nurturing Gifted and Talented Children at Key Stage 1: A Report of Action Research Project*. London: Department of Education and Skills. http://dera.ioe.ac.uk/6402/1/rr741.pdf (accessed 28th February 2017).

7) Submerged Talent and details of the Urban Scholars Programme, can be obtained from: http://content.yudu.com/A1rt97/SecEd14Apr11/resources/15.htm (accessed on 21st November 2016).

8) World-Class Problem Solving Tests were designed in 2000–2001, by the UK's Qualifications and Curriculum Authority.

9) Sheffield, L. (2009) Developing mathematical creativity – Questions may have the answer, in: Leikin, R., Berman, A. and Koichu, B. (Eds) *Creativity in Mathematics and the Education of Gifted Students*. The Netherlands: Sense Publications.

10) Dweck, C. (2006) *Mindset: The New Psychology of Success, How We Can Learn to Fulfil Our Potential*. New York: Ballantine Books.

11) A project carried out for the Mayor of London and the Department for Education, in England 2013–2015, www.talkmathstalk.co.uk, led by Valsa Koshy.

12) Alexander, R. (2008) *Learning to talk, talking to learn*. www.collaborativelearning.org/alexander.pdf (accessed on 12th November 2016).

13) Gardner, H. (2000) *Intelligence Reframed: Multiple Intelligences for the 21st Century*. New York: Basic Books.

14) Gardner, H. (1983) *Frames of Mind*. New York: Basic Books.

15) Gardner, H. (1993) *Multiple Intelligences*. New York: Basic Books.

16) Van Tassel-Baska, J. (2005) Domain-specific giftedness: Applications in school and life, in: R. Sternberg and J. Davidson (Eds) *Conceptions of Giftedness*. New York: Cambridge University Press.

17) Howe, M. (1999) *The Psychology of High Abilities*. New York: New York University Press.

18) Ericsson, K.A. (1996) *The Road to Expert Performance: Empirical Evidence from the arts and Sciences, Sports and Games*. Mahwah, N.J., USA: Erlbaum.

19) Bloom, B. (1985) Ed. *Developing talent in young people*. New York: Ballantine.

20) Koshy, V. and Robinson, N. (2006) Too long neglected: gifted young children. *European Early Childhood Education Research Journal*. 14(2):133–126.

21) Koshy, V., Pinheiro-Torres, C. and Portman Smith, C. (2012) The Landscape of Gifted and Talented Education in England and Wales: How are teachers implementing policy? *Research Papers in Education*. 27(2):167–118.

22) Montgomery, D. (2012) *Dual Exceptionality. NACE Insight*. Autumn 2012 Issue.

23) Seligman, M. (1995) *The Optimistic Child*. New York, USA: Houghton Mifflin Company.

24) Koshy, V. (1999) *Teaching Gifted Children 4–7*. London: David Fulton.

25) Tough, P. (2013) *How Children Succeed: Grit, Curiosity, and the Hidden Power of Character*. London: Random House.

Chapter 2

1) Gardner, H. (1983) *Frames of Mind*. New York: Basic Books.

2) Gardner, H. (1993) *Multiple Intelligences*. New York: Basic Books.

3) *Times Education Supplement* (2007) *How to best serve young talented 'waiters'*. Valsa Koshy 4 May 2007. https://www.tes.com/news/tes-archive/tes-publication/how-best-serve-young-talented-waiters (accessed 4th July 2017).

4) Monks, F., Heller, K and Passow, H. (2000) The study of giftedness and talent: reflections on where we are and where we are going, in K. Heller, F. Monks, R. Sternberg and R. Subotnik (Eds) *International Handbook of Giftedness and Talent*, pp. 839–863. Oxford: Pergamon.

5) Terman, L.M. (1925) *Genetic Studies of Genius: Vol. 1, Mental and Physical Traits of a Thousand Gifted Children*. Stanford: Stanford University Press.

6) Feldhusen, J. (2003) The nature of giftedness and talent and the pursuit of creative achievement and expertise. *The Journal of the National Association of Gifted Children*. 7(1):3–5.

7) George. D. (1992) *The Challenge of the Able Child*. London: David Fulton.

8) Bian, L., Leslie, S.J. and Cimpian, A. (2017) Gender stereotypes about intellectual ability emerge early and influence children's interests. *Science*. 2017 Jan 27;355(6323):389-391.

9) BBC News. (2017) *Girls lose faith in their own talents by the age of six*. http://www.bbc.co.uk/news/health-38717926 (accessed 28th February 2017).

10) Renzulli, J. (2005) The Three-Ring conception of giftedness: A developmental model for creative productivity, in: R.J. Sternberg and J.E. Davidson (Eds), *Conceptions of Giftedness*. Cambridge: Cambridge University Press.

11) Claxton, G. and Meadows, S. (2009) Brightening up: How children learn to be gifted, in: T. Balchin, B. Hymer and D. Matthews (Eds), *The Routledge International Companion to Gifted Education*. Oxford: Routledge.

12) Koshy, V. and Pinheiro-Torres, C. (2013) 'Are we being de-gifted, Miss?' Primary school gifted and talented co-ordinators' responses to the Gifted and Talented Education Policy in England. *British Educational Research Journal*. 39(6):953–978.

13) Van Tassel-Baska, J. (2005) Domain-specific giftedness: Applications in school and life, in: R. Sternberg and J. Davidson (Eds), *Conceptions of Giftedness*. New York: Cambridge University Press.

14) Sternberg, R. (2000) Giftedness as developing expertise, in: K. Heller, F. Monks, R. Sternberg and R. Subotnik (Eds), *International Handbook of Giftedness and Talent*. Oxford: Pergamon.

15) Borland, J.H. (2005) Gifted education without gifted children: The case for no conception of giftedness, in: R. Sternberg and J. Davidson (Eds), *Conceptions of Giftedness*. New York: Cambridge University Press.

16) Howe. M. (1999) *The Psychology of High Abilities*. New York: New York University Press.

17) Ericsson, K.A. (1996) *The Road to Expert Performance: Empirical Evidence from the Arts and Sciences, Sports and, Games*. Mahwah, N.J., USA: Erlbaum.

18) Her Majesty's Inspectorate. (1978) *Primary Education in England: A Survey by HM Inspections of Schools*. London: HMSO.

19) Her Majesty's Inspectorate. (1979) *Aspects of Secondary Education in England*. London: HMSO.

20) Her Majesty's Inspectorate. (1992) *Education Observed: The Education of Very Able Pupils in Maintained Schools*. London: HMSO.

21) McIntosh, D. (1994) *Exceptionally Able Children*. London: Ofsted.

22) Department for Education and Employment. (1999) *Excellence in Cities*. London: Department for Education and Employment.

23) Department for Children, Schools and Families (2008) *Identifying Gifted and Talented Learners – Getting Started*. London: Department for Children, Schools and Families.

24) Koshy, V. and Pinheiro-Torres, C. (2013) 'Are we being de-gifted, Miss?' Primary school gifted and talented co-ordinators' responses to the Gifted and Talented Education Policy in England. *British Educational Research Journal*. 39(6):953–978.

25) House of Commons (2010) *The Gifted and Talented Programme: Oral and Written Evidence. Children, School and Families Select Committee, 1 Feb 2010*. London: The Stationery Office.

26) Evans, L. (2010) 'G&T policy "inconsistent"' (Editorial) in *G&T Update*, Issue 72, March 2010.

27) Marland, S. (1972). *Education of the Gifted and Talented: Report to the Congress of the United States by the U.S. Commissioner of Education*. Washington: U.S. Government Printing Office.

28) Koshy, V. and Casey, R. (1997) *Effective Provision for Able and Exceptionally Able Children*. London: Hodder and Stoughton.

29) Dweck, C. (2006) *Mindset: The New Psychology of Success, How We Can Learn to Fulfil Our Potential*. New York: Ballantine Books.

30) Coleman, A. (2008) in *The Oxford Dictionary of Psychology*, quotes Daniel Goleman.

31) Goleman, D. (1998) *Working with Emotional Intelligence*. London: Bloomsbury.

Chapter 3

1) Lucas, B. and Claxton G. (2010) *New Kinds of Smart: How the Science of Learnable Intelligence is Changing Education: How the Science of Learnable Intelligence is Changing Education*. Maidenhead: Open University Press.

2) Thomas, L., Casey, R. and Koshy, V. (1996) The education of able and exceptionally able children in England and Wales. Paper presented at the American Educational Research Association conference. April, New York, United States of America.

3) Freeman, J. (1998) *Educating the Very Able. Current International Research*. London: Ofsted.

4) Freeman, J. (1991) *Gifted Lives: What Happens When Gifted Children Grow Up*. London: Taylor & Francis Ltd, Routledge.

5) George, D. (1992) *The Challenge of the Able Child*. London: D. Fulton.

6) Business Insider UK. *29 famous people who failed before they succeeded*. http://uk.businessinsider.com/successful-people-who-failed-at-first-2015-7?r=US&IR=T/#lt-disney-was-fired-from-the-kansas-city-star-because-his-editor-felt-he-lacked-imagination-and-had-no-good-ideas-1 (accessed 4th July 2017).

7) History of Famous people: Churchill. *10 Things You May Not Know About Winston Churchill*. www.history.com/news/10-things-you-may-not-know-about-winston-churchill (accessed 5th December 2016).

8) *The Independent* (2014). *Once upon a time, Stephen Hawking was just another schoolboy…* http://www.independent.co.uk/news/science/once-upon-a-time-stephen-hawking-was-just-another-schoolboy-9102735.html (accessed 4th July 2017).

9) Stephen Hawking. (2013) *My Brief History*. Bantam Press; First Edition edition.

10) Biography.com editors. Stephen Hawking Biography. http://www.biography.com/people/stephen-hawking-9331710 (accessed 13th December 2016).

11) Clynes, T. (2016) How to raise a genius: lessons from a 45-year study of super-smart children. *Nature*. 7 September 2016.

12) Sylva, K. (1994) School Influences of children's development. *Journal of Psychology and Psychiatry and Related Fields*. 35(1):135–179.

13) Rutter, M. and Rutter, M. (1992) *Developing Minds. Challenge and Continuity Across the Life Span*. New York: Basic Books.

14) Koshy, V., Mitchell, C. and Williams. M. (2006) *Nurturing Gifted and Talented Children at Key Stage 1: A Report of Action Research Project*. London: Department of Education and Employment. http://dera.ioe.ac.uk/6402/1/rr741.pdf (accessed 5th December 2016).

15) National Foundation for Educational Research (NFER) https://www.nfer.ac.uk (accessed 4th July 2017).

16) Gardner, H. (1983) *Frames of Mind*. New York: Basic Books.

Chapter 4

1) Alfred Binet, a French psychologist, is best known for his applied research on intelligence. Binet died in 1911; his work can be found in *Modern Ideas About Children* by Suzzane Heisler (1975), CA: Menlo Park.

2) Dweck, C. (2006) *Mindset: The New Psychology of Success, How We Can Learn to Fulfil Our Potential*. New York: Random House.

3) Vygotsky, L. (1978) *Mind in Society*. Cambridge: Harvard University Press.

4) Bloom, B.S. (1956) *Taxonomy of Educational Objectives. Volume 1*. Harlow: Longman.

5) Williams, R. (2016) Speech given by the former Archbishop of Canterbury, *Times Higher Education Supplement*, available online at: https://www.timeshighereducation.com/news/rowan-williams-decries-narrow-impact-agenda/2012743.article (accessed 15th November 2016).

Chapter 5

1) Enhancing Mathematical Learning at Key Stage 1 through talk. www.talkmathstalk.co.uk led by V. Koshy, a project carried out for the Mayor of London and the Department of Education, in England 2013–2015 (accessed 28th February 2017).

2) Vygotsky, L. (1978) *Mind in Society*. Cambridge: Harvard University Press.

3) John Flavell on Theories of Learning in Educational Psychology. http://www.demenzemedicinagenerale.net/images/mens-sana/Theories_of_Learning_in_Educational_Psychology.pdf (accessed 22nd February 2017).

4) Dweck, C. (2006) *Mindset: The New Psychology of Success, How We Can Learn to Fulfil Our Potential*. New York: Ballantine Books.

5) Tough, P. (2013) *How Children Succeed: Grit, Curiosity, and the Hidden Power of Character*. London: Random House.

6) Weaver, I.C.G., Cervoni, N., Champagne, F.A., D'Alessio, A.C., Sharma, S., Seckl, J.R., Dymov, S., Szyf, M. & Meaney, M. (2004). *Epigenetic programming by maternal behavior. Nature Neuroscience.* 7, 847–854.

Part II: Health and Wellbeing

Chapter 6

1) Adi, Y., Killoran, A., Janmohamed, K. and Stewart-Brown, S. *Systematic review of the effectiveness of interventions to promote mental wellbeing in children in primary education. Report 1: Universal approaches: non-violence related outcomes.* Coventry: University of Warwick. 2007. http://www.crd.york.ac.uk/CRDWeb/ShowRecord.asp?ID=12008008113

2) World Health Organization (WHO) (2014) *10 Facts on Mental Health.* www.who.int/features/factfiles/mental_health/mental_health_facts/en/ Updated 2014 (accessed 13th November 2016).

3) Gutman, L.M., Joshi, H., Parsonage, M. and Schoon, I. *Children of the New Century: Mental health findings from the Millennium Cohort Study.* https://www.centreformentalhealth.org.uk/children-of-the-new-century (accessed 4th July 2017).

4) The Children's Society. *Promoting positive well-being for children: A report for decision-makers in parliament, central government and local areas.* https://www.childrenssociety.org.uk/sites/default/files/tcs/promoting_positive_well-being_for_children_final.pdf (accessed 4th July 2017).

5) Office for National Statistics (2016) *Measuring National Well-being: Insights into children's mental health and well-being.* https://www.ons.gov.uk/peoplepopulationandcommunity/wellbeing/articles/measuringnationalwellbeing/2015-10-20 (accessed 25th May 2017).

6) The Children's Society. (2016) *The Good Childhood Report 2016.* https://www.childrenssociety.org.uk/sites/default/files/pcr090_mainreport_web.pdf (accessed 4th July 2017).

7) Department for Education. (2012) *The Impact of pupil behaviour and wellbeing on educational outcomes.* https://www.gov.uk/government/uploads/system/uploads/attachment_data/file/219638/DFE-RR253.pdf. November 2012 (accessed 13th November 2016).

8) Public Health England (2014) *The link between pupil health and wellbeing and attainment. A briefing for head teachers, governors and staff in education settings.* https://www.gov.uk/government/uploads/system/uploads/attachment_data/file/370686/HT_briefing_layoutvFINALvii.pdf November 2014 (accessed 13th November 2016).

9) NHS England (2015) *Future in mind: Promoting, protecting and improving our children and young people's mental health and wellbeing.* https://www.gov.uk/government/publications/improving-mental-health-services-for-young-people (accessed 13th November 2016).

10) BBC News (2017) *Mental health reforms to focus on young people, says PM.* www.bbc.co.uk/news/uk-politics-38548567 (accessed 10th January 2017).

11) Potential Plus UK (2015). *Too Much Too Soon? The Emotional and Mental Health Issues of the UK's High Learning Potential Children.* https://www.potentialplusuk.org/wp-content/uploads/2017/02/Too-much-too-soon-4-FINAL.pdf (accessed 4th July 2017).

12) Robert Jobson article in the *Evening Standard*. (2016) *Prince William's hopes for his children... and why there is no shame in feeling down*. www.standard.co.uk/news/uk/prince-williams-hopes-for-his-children-and-why-there-is-no-shame-in-feeling-down-a3346731.html. 16 September 2016 (accessed 13th November 2016).

13) Headstogether (2016) *10 Tips For Talking to Children About Their Worries*. https://www.headstogether.org.uk/10-tips-for-talking-to-kids-about-their-worries/ (accessed 4th July 2017).

14) Maslow, A.H. (1943). A theory of human motivation. *Psychological Review*. 50(4):370–396.

15) The Children's Society. *Promoting positive well-being for children*. http://childrenssociety.org.uk/what-we-do/research/well-being/publications/promoting-positive-well-being-children (accessed 13th November 2016).

16) BBC News (2013) *Stephen Fry: Suicide risk in bipolar disorder*. www.bbc.co.uk/news/health-22796593. 6 June 2013 (accessed 13th November 2016).

17) BBC News (2011) *Catherine Zeta Jones treated for bipolar disorder*. www.bbc.co.uk/news/uk-wales-13073676. 14th April 2011 (accessed 4th July 2017).

18) *OK!* (2015). *Will Young reveals anxiety disorder stopped him recognising himself*. http://www.ok.co.uk/celebrity-news/491302/will-young-reveals-anxiety-disorder. 24th October 2015 (accessed 4th July 2017).

19) *Daily Mail* (2016) *'I felt more and more isolated': Robbie Williams describes the roller coaster ride with drugs, drink and depression that almost killed him... as he gets tearful over a video of his daughter*. http://www.dailymail.co.uk/tvshowbiz/article-3934382/Robbie-Williams-describes-roller-coaster-ride-drugs-drink-depression-killed-him.html (accessed 4th July 2017).

20) Time to Change. www.time-to-change.org.uk/news-media/celebrity-supporters (accessed 13th November 2016).

21) BBC News (2008) *Is depression good for you?* http://news.bbc.co.uk/1/hi/magazine/7268496.stm (accessed 4th July 2017).

22) Greer, S.M., Goldstein, A.N., Walker, M.P. (2013) The impact of sleep deprivation on food desire in the human brain. *Nature Communications*. 4:2259.

23) Marcus, C.L., Brooks, L.J., Draper, K.A., Gozal, D., Halbower, A.C., et al. (2012) Diagnosis and management of childhood obstructive sleep apnea syndrome. *Pediatrics*. 130: 576–584.

24) Royal College of Psychiatrists. *Sleep problems in childhood and adolescence: for parents, carers and anyone who works with young people*. http://www.rcpsych.ac.uk/healthadvice/parentsandyouthinfo/parentscarers/sleepproblems.aspx (accessed 4th July 2017).

25) National Sleep Foundation. https://sleepfoundation.org/sleep-topics/children-and-sleep (accessed 13th November 2016).

26) BBC News (2017) *Sleep problems mounting in children*. http://www.bbc.co.uk/news/health-39140836 (accessed 4th July 2017).

27) NHS Choices. *Children's sleep*. http://www.nhs.uk/livewell/childrenssleep/Pages/Childrenssleephome.aspx (accessed 4th July 2017).

28) Kelly, Y., Kelly, J. and Sacker, A. (2013) Changes in bedtime schedules and behavioral difficulties in 7 year-old children. *Pediatrics*. 132(5):e1184–1193.

Chapter 7

1) Royal College of Psychiatrists. *Worries and anxieties: information for young people.* http://www.rcpsych.ac.uk/healthadvice/parentsandyouthinfo/youngpeople/worriesandanxieties.aspx (accessed 4th July 2017).

2) NHS Choices. *Anxiety in Children.* www.nhs.uk/Conditions/stress-anxiety-depression/Pages/anxiety-in-children.aspx (accessed 13th November 2016).

3) Creswell, Cathy and Willetts, Lucy (2010) *Overcoming Your Child's Fears and Worries. A Guide for Parents Using Cognitive Behavioural Techniques.* London: Robinson.

4) NHS Choices. *Cognitive Behavioural Therapy (CBT).* www.nhs.uk/conditions/cognitive-behavioural-therapy/Pages/Introduction.aspx#howitworks (accessed 4th July 2017).

5) Young Minds. www.youngminds.org.uk/ (accessed 13th November 2016).

6) Family Lives. *Listening, supportive and non-judgemental.* www.familylives.org.uk/ (accessed 13th November 2016).

7) The Child Anxiety Network. www.childanxiety.net/ (accessed 13th November 2016).

8) Dąbrowski and the gifted individual. *Positive Disintegration.* https://en.wikipedia.org/wiki/Positive_disintegration#D.C4.85browski_and_the_gifted_individual (accessed 13th November 2016).

9) Bainbridge, C. (2016) *What are Dąbrowski's Five Overexcitabilities in Gifted Children?* Why gifted kids may seem to be highly sensitive. https://www.verywell.com/dabrowskis-overexcitabilities-in-gifted-children-1449118 (accessed 13th November 2016).

10) Wolke, D., Copeland, W.E., Angold, A. and Costello, E.J. (2013) Impact of bullying in childhood on adult health, wealth, crime, and social outcomes. *Psychol Sci.* 24(10): 1958–1970.

11) Wolke, D. (2014) Economic and Social Research Council funded research. The long-term cost of bullying. Evidence briefing. http://www.esrc.ac.uk/files/news-events-and-publications/evidence-briefings/the-long-term-cost-of-bullying/ (accessed 4th July 2017).

12) Wolke, D. and Lereya, S.T. (2015) Long-term effects of bullying. *Arch Dis Child.* 100(9): 879–885.

13) Bullying UK. *What is cyberbullying?* www.bullying.co.uk/cyberbullying/what-is-cyberbullying/ (accessed 13th November 2016).

14) BBC News (2013). *Childhood bullying 'damages adult life'.* www.bbc.co.uk/news/education-23756749 (accessed 13th November 2016).

15) Copeland, W.E., Wolke, D., Lereya, S.T., Shanahan, L., Worthman, C. and Costello, E.J. (2014) Childhood bullying involvement predicts low-grade systemic inflammation into adulthood. *Proceedings of the National Academy of Sciences of the United States of America.* 111(21):7570–7575.

16) Gutman, L. and Feinstein, L. (2008a). *Children's Wellbeing in primary school: pupil and school effects*, Centre for Research on the Wider Benefits to Learning.

17) Gutman, L. and Feinstein, L. (2008b). *Pupil and School Effects on Children's Well-Being*. London: DCSF.

18) NHS Choices. *Bullying*. www.nhs.uk/Livewell/Bullying/Pages/Bullyinghome.aspx (accessed 13th November 2016).

19) Childline. https://childline.org.uk/ (accessed 13th November 2016).

20) Bullying UK. www.bullying.co.uk/ (accessed 13th November 2016).

21) Bullybusters. www.bullybusters.org.uk/ (accessed 13th November 2016).

22) Children's Hospital of Pittsburgh. *Assertiveness*. http://kidshealth.org/ChildrensHospital Pittsburgh/en/teens/assertive.html (accessed 4th July 2017).

23) Public Health England (2014) *Local action on health inequalities: Building children and young people's resilience in schools*. September 2014. https://www.gov.uk/government/uploads/system/uploads/attachment_data/file/355770/Briefing2_Resilience_in_schools_health_inequalities.pdf (accessed 13th November 2016).

24) Seligman, Martin (2007) *The Optimistic Child: A Proven Program to Safeguard Children Against Depression and Build Lifelong Resilience*. US Imports. Reprint edition.

25) PSHE Association. https://www.pshe-association.org.uk/ (accessed 13th November 2016).

26) PSHE Association (2015) *Teacher Guidance: Preparing to Teach about Mental Health and Emotional Wellbeing*. PSHE Association guidance funded by the Department for Education. March 2015.

27) Stewart-Brown, Sarah. NHS Choices. *Stress Anxiety and Depression. Five steps to mental wellbeing*. www.nhs.uk/Conditions/stress-anxiety-depression/Pages/improve-mental-wellbeing.aspx (accessed 13th November 2016).

28) New Economics Foundation (NEF) (2008) *Five ways to wellbeing*. www.fivewaystowellbeing.org/ (accessed 13th November 2016).

29) The Children's Society (2013) *Ways to well-being*. www.childrenssociety.org.uk/what-we-do/research/well-being/ways-well-being (accessed 13th November 2016).

30) The Children's Society (2013) *How to support your child's well-being*. www.childrenssociety.org.uk/sites/default/files/tcs/good_childhood_report_2013_final.pdf (accessed 13th November 2016).

31) Matthews, Dona (2014) Blog: *Play Outside! Twelve Ways to Health, Happiness, Intelligence, and Creativity, and to Environmental Sustainability*. https://donamatthews.wordpress.com/2014/04/24/play-outside-twelve-ways-to-health-happiness-intelligence-and-creativity-and-to-environmental-sustainability/ (accessed 13th November 2016).

32) Ofsted (2008) *Raising standards improving lives. Learning outside the classroom: How far should you go?* www.lotc.org.uk/wp-content/uploads/2010/12/Ofsted-Report-Oct-2008.pdf (accessed 13th November 2016).

Chapter 8

1) Maslow, A.H. (1943). A theory of human motivation. *Psychological Review*. 50(4):370–396.

2) *National Child Measurement Programme – England*, 2015–16. Publication date: November 2016. http://content.digital.nhs.uk/searchcatalogue?productid=23381&q=national+child+measurement+programme&sort=Relevance&size=10&page=1#top (accessed 13th February 2017).

3) World Health Organization. *Childhood overweight and obesity*. www.who.int/topics/obesity/en/ (accessed 13th November 2016).

4) NHS Choices. *BMI Healthy weight calculator*. http://www.nhs.uk/Tools/Pages/Healthy weightcalculator.aspx (accessed 4th July 2017).

5) Change4Life. *Your child's weight*. https://www.nhs.uk/change4life-beta/be-food-smart#YTOJV63g4YfumQDM.97 (accessed 6th July 2017).

6) Public Health England (2016). *The Eatwell Guide*. Helping you eat a healthy, balanced diet. https://www.gov.uk/government/publications/the-eatwell-guide (accessed 13th November 2016).

7) Public Health England (2016) *The Eatwell Plate*. https://www.gov.uk/government/uploads/system/uploads/attachment_data/file/510366/UPDATED_Eatwell-23MAR2016_England.pdf (accessed 13th November 2016).

8) Bradbury, K.E., Appleby, P.N. and Key, T.J. (2014) Fruit, vegetable, and fiber intake in relation to cancer risk: findings from the European Prospective Investigation into Cancer and Nutrition (EPIC). *Am. J. Clin. Nutr.* 10(Suppl 1):394S–398S.

9) D'Anci, K.E., Constant, F. and Rosenberg, I.H. (2006) Hydration and cognitive function in children. *Nutr Rev.* 64(10 Pt 1):457–464.

10) Bar-David, Y., Urkin, J. and Kozminsky, E. (2005) The effect of voluntary dehydration on cognitive functions of elementary school children. *Acta. Paediatr.* 94(11):1667–1673.

11) Fadda, R., Rapinett, G., Grathwohl, D., Paris, I.M., Fanari, R., Calò, C.M. and Schmitt, J. (2012) Effects of drinking supplementary water at school on cognitive performance in children. *Appetite*. 59(3):730–737.

12) Edmonds, C.J. and, Burford, D. (2009) Should children drink more water? The effects of drinking water on cognition in children. *Appetite*. 52(3):776–779. doi: 10.1016/j.appet.2009.02.010.

13) Shirreffs, S.M., Merson, S.J., Fraser, S.M. and Archer, D.T. (2004) The effects of fluid restriction on hydration status and subjective feelings in man. *Br. J. Nutr.* 91(6):951–958.

14) BBC News (2016) *Sugar tax: How will it work?* www.bbc.co.uk/news/health-35824071 (accessed 13th November 2016).

15) Dimbleby, Henry and Vincent, John (2013) *The School Food Plan*. July 2013. https://www.gov.uk/government/uploads/system/uploads/attachment_data/file/251020/The_School_Food_Plan.pdf (accessed 13th November 2016).

16) European Food Safety Authority. (2010) Scientific opinion on dietary reference values for water. *EFSA Journal*. 8(3):1459 [48 pp.]. www.efsa.europa.eu/en/efsajournal/pub/1459 (accessed 13th November 2016).

17) Martínez-González, M.A., Salas-Salvadó, J., Estruch, R., Corella, D., Fitó, M. and Ros, E. (2015) PREDIMED Investigators. Benefits of the Mediterranean diet: Insights from the PREDIMED Study. *Prog. Cardiovasc. Dis.* 58(1):50–60.

18) NHS Choices. *Oily fish: mighty omega 3 or codswollop?* www.nhs.uk/Livewell/superfoods/Pages/is-oily-fish-a-superfood.aspx (accessed 13th November 2016).

19) NHS Choices. *Food labels.* www.nhs.uk/Livewell/Goodfood/Pages/food-labelling.aspx#Nutrition.

20) World Health Organization (WHO) (2014). *WHO opens public consultation on draft sugars guideline.* March 2014. www.who.int/mediacentre/news/notes/2014/consultation-sugar-guideline/en/ (accessed 13th November 2016).

21) de la Hunty, A. and Ashwell, M. (2006) Are people who regularly eat breakfast cereals slimmer than those who don't? A systematic review of the evidence. *Nutr. Bull.* 32:118–128.

22) Hansen, K. and Joshi, H. (2008) *Millennium Cohort Study Third Survey: A User's Guide to Initial Findings*, p. 162. London: Centre for Longitudinal Studies, Institute of Education.

23) Public Health England (2013) *Breakfast and cognition. Review of the literature.* https://www.gov.uk/government/uploads/system/uploads/attachment_data/file/256398/Breakfast_and_cognition_review_FINAL_publication_formatted.pdf (accessed 4th July 2017).

24) Public Health England. (2017) Press release: New Change4Life campaign encourages parents to 'Be Food Smart'. https://www.gov.uk/government/news/new-change4life-campaign-encourages-parents-to-be-food-smart

25) BBC News (2017). *Kids devouring too much 'breakfast sugar' warning.* www.bbc.co.uk/news/health-38467861 (accessed 3rd January 2017).

26) Change4Life. *Get the New Be Food Smart App.* https://www.nhs.uk/change4life-beta/be-food-smart#YTOJV63g4YfumQDM.97 (accessed 6th January 2017).

27) Department for Education. *School Food in England.* https://www.gov.uk/government/uploads/system/uploads/attachment_data/file/551813/School_food_in_England.pdf (accessed 13th November 2016).

28) Street, C. and Kenway, P. (1999) *Food for Thought: Breakfast Clubs and their Challenges.* London: New Policy Institute.

29) Ells, L.J., Hillier, F.C., Shucksmith, J., Crawley, H., Harbige, L., Shield, J., Wiggins, A. and Summerbell, C.D. (2008) A systematic review of the effect of dietary exposure that could be achieved through normal dietary intake on learning and performance of school-aged children of relevance to UK schools. *Br. J. Nutr.* 100(5):927–936.

30) Edefonti, V., Rosato, V., Parpinel, M., Nebbia, G., Fiorica, L., Fossali, E., Ferraroni, M., Decarli, A. and Agostoni, C. (2014) The effect of breakfast composition and energy contribution on cognitive and academic performance: a systematic review. *Am. J. Clin. Nutr.* 100(2):626–656.

31) World Health Organization. *Physical activity and young people. Recommended levels of physical activity for children aged 5–17 years.* www.who.int/dietphysicalactivity/factsheet_young_people/en/ (accessed 13th November 2016).

32) National Institute for Care and Health Excellence (NICE) (2009). *Physical activity for children and young people.* https://www.nice.org.uk/Guidance/PH17 (accessed 13th November 2016).

33) NHS Choices. *Physical activity guidelines for children and young people.* www.nhs.uk/Livewell/fitness/Pages/physical-activity-guidelines-for-young-people.aspx (accessed 13th November 2016).

34) Public Health England (2014) *The link between pupil health and wellbeing and attainment A briefing for head teachers, governors and staff in education settings.* https://www.gov.uk/government/uploads/system/uploads/attachment_data/file/370686/HT_briefing_layoutvFINALvii.pdf. November 2014 (accessed 13th November 2016).

35) Booth, J., Leary, S., Joinson, C., Ness, A., Tomporowski, P., Boyle, J. and Reilly, J. (2014). Associations between objectively measured physical activity and academic attainment in adolescents from a UK cohort. *British Journal of Sports Medicine.* 48:265–270.

36) Royal College of Psychiatrists. *Physical activity and mental health.* www.rcpsych.ac.uk/healthadvice/treatmentswellbeing/physicalactivity.aspx (accessed 13th November 2016).

37) Levine, J.A. (2002) Non-exercise activity thermogenesis (NEAT). *Best Pract. Res. Clin. Endocrinol. Metab.* 16(4):679–702.

38) Levine, J.A., Vander Weg, M.W., Hill, J.O. and Klesges, R.C. (2006) Non-exercise activity thermogenesis. The Crouching Tiger Hidden Dragon of societal weight gain. *Arteriosclerosis, Thrombosis, and Vascular Biology.* 26:729–736. Originally published March 23, 2006.

Appendices

Elizabeth Koshy

Appendix 1: Definitions of Health and the Different Wellbeing Domains

The words *health* and *wellbeing* are not always used consistently. The concepts can overlap and this can create some confusion. This Appendix provides the globally recognised definitions used by the World Health Organization (WHO) within text boxes.

Health is a *spectrum* which ranges from being *well* to *poor health*, or *illness*.

The word health has a very broad meaning and encompasses physical and mental health.

Health

The WHO defines *health*, by which it means *good health*, as: *'A state of complete physical, mental and social wellbeing and not merely the absence of disease or infirmity'*.[1]

Wellbeing

The WHO proposes that: *'wellbeing exists in two dimensions, subjective and objective'* and that *'it comprises an individual's experience of their life as well as a comparison of life circumstances with social norms and values'*.[2]

As the American Centers for Disease Control and Prevention (CDC) highlight there is no consensus around a universal definition of (good) *wellbeing*, but there is general acceptance that it includes, as a minimum, *'the presence of positive emotions and moods (e.g. contentment, happiness), the absence of negative emotions (e.g. depression, anxiety), satisfaction with life and positive functioning'*.[3] The CDC also promotes a simple way of thinking about (good) wellbeing as: viewing *'life positively and feeling good'*.[3] Furthermore, The Mental Health Foundation and the Faculty of Public Health similarly highlight that (positive) *mental wellbeing* concerns *'feeling good'* and *'functioning well'*, which are 'subjective' measures, that vary between individuals. Mental wellbeing focusses on the more *positive* end of the mental health spectrum.[4] The report, 'Better Mental Health for All: A public health approach to mental health improvement' (2016), states that emotional wellbeing is frequently used interchangeably with mental wellbeing.[4] However, in this book I have used a more specific definition of emotional wellbeing.

An individual child can be in poor health but have good mental wellbeing. For example, a child in hospital might be in poor physical health but be surrounded by a loving family and have trust in the doctors and nurses who treat her. Her mental wellbeing would be positive despite being physically ill. The opposite may also occur where a child may be in good health but he has poor mental wellbeing, for example, if there are external factors such as adverse school or home circumstances.

The national mental health charity, MIND, which primarily focusses on adults, highlights that mental wellbeing is a dynamic and fluid state, and that it can alter from one moment to the next, from day to day, month to month and year to year.[5] The organisation goes further by describing what (good) mental wellbeing represents and this has relevance for children too. Some of the factors MIND refers to, include:

'…being able to express a range of feelings and emotions; feeling relatively confident in yourself and having positive self-esteem, building and maintaining good relationships with others, feeling part of and engaged in the world around you and coping with stresses and challenges of daily life'.[5]

Mental health

According to the WHO (2014), (good) mental health is: *'A state of wellbeing in which every individual realises his or her own potential, can cope with the normal stresses of life, can work productively and fruitfully, and is able to make a contribution to her or his community'.[6]*

Therefore, the WHO's definition of mental health is potentially interchangeable with what I and others call mental wellbeing.

Mental illness or *mental ill-health* can present differently in children to the way it does in adults.[7] It can manifest as behavioural and conduct problems, including Attention Deficit Hyperactivity Disorder (ADHD) or Oppositional Defiant Disorder (ODD), as well as emotional conditions, such as anxiety or depression. These conditions can also be suggestive of underlying issues which could be environmental (such as adverse family circumstances or relationships) or developmental, for example, Autistic Spectrum Disorder (ASD).[7]

The National Institute for Health and Care Excellence (NICE) guidelines provide the following more detailed definitions of emotional, psychological and social wellbeing:[8]

- *(good) emotional wellbeing* – *'includes being happy and confident and not anxious or depressed'.*

- *(good) psychological wellbeing* – *'includes the ability to be autonomous, problem-solve, manage emotions, experience empathy, be resilient and attentive'.*

- *(good) social wellbeing* – *'has good relationships with others and does not have behavioural problems, that is, they are not disruptive, violent or a bully'.*

Physical wellbeing represents an individual's feelings about his or her own health (e.g. feeling very healthy and full of energy, or the opposite).[3]

Wellbeing is often used in a narrower sense as shorthand for mental and social wellbeing to express how people feel about themselves and their social interactions. The Office for National Statistics, for instance, measures personal wellbeing through a range of questions concerning how individuals feel about their lives.[7] This may make interesting reading.

Additional References for Appendix 1

1) World Health Organization (WHO). *WHO Definition of Health.* http://who.int/about/definition/en/print.html (accessed 13th November 2016).

2) World Health Organization (WHO) *Measurement of and target-setting for well-being: an initiative by the WHO Regional Office for Europe.* Second meeting of the expert group Paris, France, 25–26 June 2012. http://www.euro.who.int/__data/assets/pdf_file/0009/181449/e96732.pdf (accessed 28th February 2017).

3) Centers for Disease Control and Prevention. *Well-being concepts.* https://www.cdc.gov/hrqol/wellbeing.htm (accessed 13th February 2017).

4) Faculty of Public Health and Mental Health Foundation (2016) *Better Mental Health for All: A Public Health Approach to Mental Health Improvement.* London.

5) MIND. For better mental health. www.mind.org.uk/information-support/tips-for-everyday-living/wellbeing#.WDLMCIXXKUl (accessed 13th November 2016).

6) World Health Organization (WHO) (2014) *Mental Health: a state of wellbeing*. www.who.int/features/factfiles/mental_health/en/ (accessed 13th November 2016).

7) Office for National Statistics. *Measuring National Well-being: Insights into children's mental health and well-being*. https://www.ons.gov.uk/peoplepopulationandcommunity/wellbeing/articles/measuringnationalwellbeing/2015-10-20#bullying (accessed 21st May 2017).

8) National Institute for Health and Care Excellence (NICE) (2013) *Social and emotional wellbeing for children and young people*. https://www.nice.org.uk/advice/lgb12/chapter/introduction (accessed 13th November 2016).

Appendix 2: Additional Information on Food

This section provides additional information on the different food groups that were outlined in Chapter 8.

Carbohydrates

About a third of the *Eatwell Guide* (see Chapter 8) plate should comprise a variety of starchy foods. Starchy foods are our main source of carbohydrates; they are an important source of energy and provide a range of nutrients in our diet, including: vitamins, iron, fibre and calcium.

There are two types of carbohydrates:

- *Simple* carbohydrates, which either require very little digestion or none at all, and therefore reach the bloodstream quickly. This means their energy is released very quickly too. They produce a surge in blood sugar. This fast energy release can be beneficial just before undertaking exercise, when it is quickly utilised for energy, but can be detrimental in many other contexts. The surge can lead to a short-lived energy peak followed by a sharp drop in energy. This can result in *challenging* behaviour, including irritability and poor concentration – obviously not ideal in a classroom (or at home!). Simple carbohydrates release energy very quickly and there can be a subsequent sudden dip. Simple sugars can be found in processed foods, such as cakes and biscuits, as well as many drinks.

- *Complex* carbohydrates are digested more slowly and release energy gradually. Therefore, complex carbohydrates are generally preferable to simple ones for most situations during the day. Complex carbohydrates include brown bread, rice, potatoes and pasta. Wholegrain (brown) varieties are preferable to processed (white) ones, as they release energy more gradually and can be better for our bowels and blood cholesterol.

Protein

Protein is important to help your child's body function, repair and grow. Protein is a component of every single cell in the human body. It is needed to make hormones, enzymes and other chemicals in the body. Protein is important for skin, hair, nails, muscle, cartilage and ligaments, as well as our blood. Sources of protein include dairy products, fish and poultry (such as chicken and turkey), Quorn™, tofu, beans and pulses, nuts and seeds.

Fats

The word *fat* has a negative association for many, yet certain types of fat are essential for our health and wellbeing. Saturated fats need to be eaten in moderation. There are also trans fats, which our bodies do not require to function, and which are typically found in processed and fried food. Healthy fats include monosaturated fatty acids and polyunsaturated fatty acid (PUFA) rich food.

- *Saturated fats* (in butter, hard cheese, cream and fatty meats) may raise blood cholesterol levels, which can contribute to clogging up your arteries and can increase the likelihood of heart disease and stroke in later years. So, as your child grows older, particularly in teenage years, they will need to start thinking about eating these foods in moderation.

- *Trans fats* (in some cakes, pastries, biscuits and deep-fried food) occur naturally in small quantities in dairy foods and meats but most trans fats are industrially produced. Artificial trans fats form during a process called hydrogenation, which makes oil more solid (known as hardening). This type of fat, known as hydrogenated fat, can be used for frying or as an ingredient in processed foods. So, avoid foods which have hydrogenated fat on their list of ingredients. Artificial trans fats are used to enhance the flavour, texture and shelf-life of some processed foods, such as cakes and biscuits.Trans fats have a similar negative effect as saturated fats in our bodies and may contribute to high cholesterol levels and therefore an increased risk of heart disease and stroke in later years. There has been a lot of media attention surrounding them and many manufacturers are now removing trans fats from their products.

- *Monounsaturated fats* (in olive oil and rapeseed oils, some nuts, including brazil nuts, and various seeds) can help to reduce Low-Density Lipoprotein (LDL) cholesterol (LDL is one of the *baddies* in the cholesterol family).

- *Polyunsaturated fatty acids* (PUFAs) (in sunflower and soya oil and spreads from these oils, nuts, seeds and fish) provide essential fatty acids (including omega-3) and are important for our body.

Minerals

Our bodies require many minerals to function well. In recent years, iron, calcium, zinc and magnesium have received particular attention in both research and the media.

Iron is an important mineral that is required to carry oxygen in haemoglobin within the red blood cells. It is through this process that oxygen reaches all the cells. Iron deficiency anaemia can particularly affect children aged under 5 years and girls who have started menstruating. Red meat, nuts, spinach, fortified cereals and beans are sources of iron. Vitamin C-rich food consumed with iron-rich food, increases the absorption of iron, so try, for instance, to give fresh fruit (high in vitamin C) with an egg (which is high in iron), to boost the iron absorption.

Zinc is needed to make enzymes and new cells, it helps with wound healing and the immune system, and it helps process carbohydrate, protein and fat in food. Zinc can be found in dairy products, some cereal products and meat.

Calcium is essential for bones and teeth, as well as muscle contractions and even our heart beating. Dairy products, including milk, cheese and yogurts are good sources of this mineral.

Magnesium, like calcium, is important for strong teeth and bones, and is involved in helping to turn food into energy. It can be found in green, leafy vegetables, nuts and seeds.

Vitamins

Vitamins are essential for our overall health. Vitamin A helps the body's immune system to fight off infections and illness, and it is also important for helping night vision; the B vitamins are particularly important for the body's nervous system, skin and eyes; vitamin C helps to maintain healthy bones, cartilage, blood vessels and skin, and it also helps with wound healing; vitamin D's key role is in maintaining healthy bones, teeth and muscles; vitamin E is very important for the immune system too; and finally, vitamin K is concerned with aiding blood clotting, which enables wounds to heal.

Although all the vitamins are very important, I am only going to focus on vitamin D, which has received considerable research and media focus in recent years. Vitamin D is an essential nutrient that helps to control the amount of calcium and phosphate in our blood, which, in turn, are responsible for healthy bones and teeth. There are numerous research studies that are investigating the potential role of vitamin D to reduce the likelihood of developing a number of conditions. Some of these studies include examining vitamin D levels in relation to different types of cancer, multiple sclerosis, high blood pressure and diabetes mellitus (types 1 and 2). However, it is important to point out that only robust studies should be relied upon for guidance and recommendations.

Most children (and adults) obtain little vitamin D from their diet. There are only a few natural foods that contain significant amounts of vitamin D, such as oily fish and eggs. Some foods are fortified with small amounts of vitamin D (e.g. margarine and some breakfast cereals). All infant formula milks are fortified with vitamin D (breast milk generally contains little vitamin D). Cow's milk is not fortified in the UK. Vitamin D supplementation, in the form of vitamin drops, is recommended for children aged under 5 years.

Vitamin D is predominantly made by our body, under the skin, in reaction to sunlight. However, vitamin D can only be effectively produced in our skin when the sun is high in the sky. Therefore, in most of the UK, from November to February, and in Scotland, from October to March, vitamin D production is restricted through reduced sun exposure. During the other months of the year, most children aged five years and above can potentially obtain enough vitamin D from sunlight when they are outdoors. Low vitamin D status is a problem among some minority ethnic groups, including those of South Asian, African and African Caribbean origin, because of pigmentation of their skin colour acting as a 'barrier', as most vitamin D is made in the skin when it is exposed to the sun.

Dame Sally Davies, the Chief Medical Officer for England, voiced concerns that children seem to be more inactive these days and spend more time indoors, for example, playing computer games, and not enough time outdoors, which places them at increased risk of developing rickets from lack of sun exposure to produce vitamin D.[1]

To produce enough vitamin D, your child's skin does not need to be exposed to the sun for long periods. Particularly take care during the peak times (between 11am and 3pm). The peak times are when the sun's rays are most intense and when there is the greatest risk of sun damage or even being burnt. Sun overexposure may increase the risk of skin cancers in later life. If you are interested in finding out about skin types do look at the article, 'Am I at risk of sunburn' on Cancer Research UK's website.[2]

Sun creams may help to prevent damage caused from excess sun exposure. However, it is a fine balance! As Professor Alastair Sutcliffe, a consultant paediatrician at University College London Hospitals, has highlighted, aside from children typically spending more time indoors in recent years, the overuse of sunblock could also be a contributing factor to the increasing number of children with vitamin D deficiency.[1]

Children with vitamin D deficiency may exhibit some of the following symptoms and signs – aches and pains, delayed walking, rickets with bowed legs, knock knees, poor growth and muscle weakness.

Do explore the NHS Choices website which discusses vitamin D, to see if your child may be at risk of low vitamin D levels and what you can do to address this.

Additional Information on Omega-3

Some adults and children believe they become more alert and find it easier to concentrate if they eat more oily fish, for others it does not make much of a difference. Interest still lies in whether omega-3 fatty acids have potential beneficial effects on a range of conditions in children, including concentration, memory, learning and behaviour among children.

Polyunsaturated Fatty Acids (PUFAs), including omega-3, have been suggested by some small studies to help conditions such as the autistic spectrum disorder (ASD) and Attention Deficit Hyperactivity Disorder (ADHD). However, an analysis by the Cochrane Group (which rigorously assesses existing medical evidence for and against different treatments and therapies) suggests that there is currently no high-quality evidence to confirm that omega-3 supplementation can help the core and associated symptoms of ASD (James *et al.*, 2011).[3] Another Cochrane Group analysis, similarly, found no clear evidence of a positive effect of PUFAs for the symptoms of

ADHD (Gillies *et al.*, 2012);[4] in fact, most of the studies analysed showed no benefit. Finally, another study by the Cochrane Group of children with specific learning disorders (Tan *et al.*, 2016) could not find sufficient evidence of benefit of PUFAs for these children.[5] Therefore, the findings highlight that large, well-designed studies are still needed to evaluate any potential benefit of omega-3, and other PUFAs, for different functions and conditions among children before any firm recommendations can be given.

Some parents I have met are convinced that omega-3 supplementation helps their children while others feel it has been a waste of effort or money. If you are considering boosting your child's PUFAs intake, one suggestion might be to trial it for a month to see if you, or your child, notice any changes. This might particularly be worth a try if your child has any attention or behavioural issues. However, because of the potential issue of a *placebo effect*, ideally, you should not tell anyone, in advance, so as not to influence or bias their thinking! The *placebo effect* represents a (beneficial) effect in an individual following the administration of a treatment (or intervention) that arises from beliefs and expectations of the treatment rather than from the actual treatment itself. You may also contemplate not going into specific detail, with your child, about the potential benefits, to avoid them directly experiencing the *placebo effect* too! Wait a month and then ask your child, your child's teacher and others, if they have noticed any *specific* changes and ask them to outline those changes, without inadvertently encouraging them to say what you want to hear!

There is currently a lack of good quality evidence supporting the benefit of omega-3 supplementation for specific problems. However, children's (and adults') diets are typically low in omega-3 and humans have limited ability to synthesise omega-3 fatty acids; therefore, we should all make a conscious effort to include them in our diets, potentially to improve aspects of our health. Ideally, increase your child's PUFA levels by modifying their diet, which will include additional PUFAs (i.e not only omega-3). So, a take-home message is to remember to encourage your child to eat more oily fish, nuts and seeds to boost omega-3 and other PUFA levels.

Additional References for Appendix 2

1) *The Telegraph* (2015) *Video games linked to return of rickets among children.* http://www.telegraph. co.uk/news/health/11548378/Video-games-linked-to-return-of-rickets-among-children. html (accessed 1st May 2017).

2) Cancer Research UK. *Am I at risk of sunburn?* http://www.cancerresearchuk.org/about-cancer/causes-of-cancer/sun-uv-and-cancer/am-i-at-risk-of-sunburn (accessed 2nd July 2017).

3) James, S., Montgomery, P. and Williams, K. (2011) Omega-3 fatty acids supplementation for autism spectrum disorders (ASD). *Cochrane Database of Systematic Reviews* 2011, Issue 11. Art. No.: CD007992. DOI: 10.1002/14651858.CD007992.pub2.

4) Gillies, D., Sinn, J.K.H., Lad, S.S., Leach, M.J. and Ross, M.J. (2012) Polyunsaturated fatty acids (PUFA) for attention deficit hyperactivity disorder (ADHD) in children and adolescents. *Cochrane Database of Systematic Reviews* 2012, Issue 7. Art. No.: CD007986. DOI: 10.1002/14651858.CD007986.pub2.

5) Tan, M., Ho, J.J. and Teh, K. (2016) Polyunsaturated fatty acids (PUFAs) for children with specific learning disorders. *Cochrane Database of Systematic Reviews* 2016, Issue 9. Art. No.: CD009398. DOI: 10.1002/14651858.CD009398.pub3.

Further Testimonials

This book is an excellent summary of the main theories and approaches towards identifying and supporting gifted and talented children. Written for parents, it provides real life case studies and examples from the extensive work done by both authors to enable parents to find and nurture their child's amazing gifts and talents.

The book stresses the importance of taking a holistic approach towards bringing up children; focussing on all aspects of their needs; educational, social, emotional, psychological and physical. It encourages parents to ask 'What are the gifts and talents of my child?' rather than 'Is my child gifted and talented?'

Focussing on the characteristics of the child rather than whether or not they are 'gifted and talented' enables the authors to bypass the debate about what is meant by the term gifted and talented. This debate has run for over a hundred years and has prevented the gifts and talents of countless children from being identified and nurtured in the right way. It is an approach we take in Potential Plus UK and which has enabled us to provide very practical support to thousands of children since 1967.

I would definitely recommend this resource to parents and also to the professionals who work with them.

Denise Yates
Chief Executive, Potential Plus UK (The operating name of The National Association for Gifted Children)

It is very refreshing to read a book written for parents, carers and grandparents supplying them with plentiful practical approaches to ponder anew their children's special gift. Recognising giftedness is taken into the realm of the family as partners and no longer limiting it to the domain of teachers and schools.

I wholeheartedly endorse this mother and daughter, co-authors', methodology. Valsa Koshy, Professor of Education and Elizabeth Koshy, Medical Doctor, effectively communicate a broad spectrum of theoretical findings and research on giftedness and translate these into practical strategies. One such example is they illustrate how to draw a web of attributes to help parents and others see each child uniquely and thereby break down some of the complexities involved in understanding and recognising giftedness.

Elizabeth Koshy's passion to help parents enhance their child's potential and happiness successfully provides essential information on components of a healthy diet and lifestyle and this convincingly and very effectively places physical as well as emotional wellbeing as foundational in a child realising her or his potential.

Valsa Koshy's passion is to train and empower children to be in charge of their learning. It is clear from her relationships with numerous youngsters she has encountered through her work, at Brunel University, as a leader in gifted and talented education, as the founder of the Urban Scholars' Programme, that she demonstrates her ability as a teacher to connect with students so they are able to express their giftedness in different ways.

Teachers do not work in isolation but as partners with parents and others to help shape each student's whole development or wellbeing, including particular giftedness. This book enables parents, carers and grandparents to become more active as partners with teachers and educators in joining their youngster's journey in giftedness. Along the way, a paradigm shift begins to occur in redefining what giftedness is. It is an exciting journey and one I recommend joining.

Dr Elizabeth Day
Headteacher, Oldfield Primary School, Ealing

*   *   *

Being a parent or carer is both rewarding and challenging. Their involvement in their child's development is crucial. The authors have a wealth of experience and expertise that have enabled them to produce a book which provides useful and effective insight into various elements which should help parents, carers and grandparents to both recognise the important role they have and to take practical steps in supporting the development of their child's own special gifts and talents, including developing life skills. I especially like the fact that the authors do not concentrate solely on developing potential, but also recognise the importance of mental and physical health and wellbeing and happiness. With its clear, accessible style, ideas and action points, this book is an essential companion for all parents, carers and grandparents who want to do their best to support their child in reaching their own unique full potential.

Susan Capel
Emeritus Professor of Sports Sciences at Brunel University

*   *   *

Every child has a gift or talent – that's at the heart of this book! Aimed at parents and grandparents, the authors – not only experts in their fields but parents and grandparents themselves – offer a refreshingly new perspective on the conventional definition of 'gifts and talents', explaining clearly how to recognise these in your child and nurture them. Professor Valsa Koshy and Doctor Elizabeth Koshy base their writing on a wealth of experience in their respective fields of education and health, supplying numerous, illustrative case studies; the authors offer clear guidance to help you discover your child's gifts and talents – largely, by simply engaging with them in everyday conversation! – and outline how to provide the best environment to ensure his or her future success.

Valerie Leech
Mother and grandmother

We are both passionate about enriching children's lives. If you have any helpful comments or would like to provide examples or case histories for our website (we can anonymise them, if you prefer), please contact us through our website:

www.enrichchildrenslives.com